Penguin Book 2502

The Penguin Book of Lost Worlds · 2

Leonard Cottrell, born in 1913 at Tettenhall, near Wolverhampton, is the author of twenty-five books, principally on archaeology and history and most of which have been published in the United States and Europe as well as in Britain. Among his best-known works are *The Bull of Minos*, *The Lost Pharaohs*, *The Anvil of Civilisation*, and *The Lion Gate*.

Educated at King Edward's Grammar School, Birmingham, he decided, while still at school, to become a writer. He first moved through advertising and journalism to the B.B.C. where, from 1942 to 1959, he wrote and produced many documentary programmes both for radio and television. His lifelong interest in archaeology and history eventually led him to write B.B.C. programmes and then books on these subjects. His first book on archaeology, *The Lost Pharaohs*, was published in 1949.

Leonard Cottrell regards his role as a professional writer as that of interpreter between the professional archaeologist and the informed layman, and tries to please the latter without offending the former. He resigned from the B.B.C. in 1959 in order to concentrate on writing and lives with his wife, a poet, in Sussex.

The Penguin Book of LOST WORLDS

Leonard Cottrell

Volume Two

Crete, Mycenae, Anatolia and Etruria

Penguin Books Ltd, Harmondsworth, Middlesex, England
Penguin Books Australia Ltd, Ringwood, Victoria, Australia

English-language edition of *The Horizon Book of Lost Worlds*
first published in the U.S.A. by
American Heritage Publishing Co., Inc., 1962

This shortened edition published as
The Penguin Book of Lost Worlds (two volumes)
by Penguin Books 1966

Made and printed in Great Britain by
Jarrold & Sons Ltd, Norwich
Set in Monotype Baskerville

Design by Burns/Price

FRONTISPIECE: The Lion Gate, Mycenae

Contents

Names and Dates

The past leads us to places with strange names and introduces us to people whose names are even stranger. In many cases there is no general agreement, even among scholars, as to how these should be spelled. The spelling used in these pages follows what seemed to be the most common usage and the simplest forms, with every effort to maintain reasonable consistency. So too there is often disagreement among the most knowledgeable authorities in the matter of dates. The chronology of the ancient world is in a constant state of flux; dates are more frequently than not interdependent, and when one is changed in the light of new discoveries, in time – sometimes slowly and erratically through the medium of scholarly publications – scores of others are dislocated from their tentatively established positions. Here again, in the chart on pages 8 and 9 and throughout the text, a reasonable consistency in relation to the most generally accepted and qualified opinion has been aimed at, but in a great many cases, the dates that are indicated must still be considered only approximate.

TIME CHART

EGYPT		MESOPOTAMIA		CRETE AND MAINLAN
Predynastic Period				
Old Kingdom	**3100–2160**	**Jemdet Naṣr Period**	**3200–3000**	
Union of Egypt	3100	Rise of Sumerian city-states	before 3000	
		Early Dynastic Period	**3000–2370**	**Rise of Cretan Civilization**
Third Dynasty	2670–2600			Neolithic settlement at Dimini
Step Pyramid	2650			
Cheops' Pyramid	2575	Royal Tombs of Ur	2500	
		Sargon	*c.* 2370	
Period of Anarchy	2160–2133	**Sumerian Revival**	**2230–2000**	
		Building of great Ur ziggurat	2100	
Middle Kingdom	**2133–1625**	**Old Babylonian Period**	**2000–1595**	**Mycenaeans Enter Greece**
		Age of Mari	*c.* 1800	
		Hammurabi	1792–1750	**Height of Cretan Culture**
Rise of Osiris cult				Building of great palaces
				Minoan domination of the sea
Hyksos Domination	1700–1567			Development of Linear A scri
New Kingdom	**1567–1085**	Hittites sack Babylon	1595	Grave circles at Mycenae
Eighteenth Dynasty	1567–1320	**Middle Babylonian Period**	**after 1595**	
				Development of Linear B scri
Empire of Tuthmosis III	1482–1450			**Mycenaeans Rule in Crete**
		Kassites rule Babylon		Destruction of palaces
Akhenaten	1379–1361			and fall of Minoan civilizatio
Tutankhamen	1361–1352			Mycenaean maritime suprem
Ramesses II	1304–1237			
Temples of Karnak				
and Abu Simbel				Trojan War
Exodus of the Hebrews	1240			Fall of Mycenaean centres
Great Invasion of Sea Peoples	1191			
		Assyrian Period	**1115–612**	**Dorian Invasion**
Late Period	**1085–525**	Conquests of Tiglath-pileser I	1115–1077	Final destruction of Mycenae
				Dark Age
Assyrians conquer Egypt	671	Height of Assyrian power	875–630	
Saite Period	664–525	Fall of Nineveh	612	Homer
		Neo-Babylonian Period	**612–538**	
		Nebuchadnezzar II	*c.* 600	**Classical Age of Greece**
Persian Domination	**525–404**	**Persian Rule**	**538–331**	Persians invade Greece
Herodotus visits Egypt	*c.* 450	Herodotus visits Babylon	*c.* 450	Herodotus
Alexander the Great conquers Egypt	332	Alexander conquers Babylon	331	Alexander the Great
Ptolemaic Period	**323–30**			
Cleopatra	69–30			

REECE	ANATOLIA AND THE LEVANT		OTHERS		
					3000
0–1900					
2700					
	Egypt trades with Byblos	2600			
	Troy II	2500–2250	**Indus Valley Civilization**	**2500–1500**	
	Alaja Huyuk	2400–2200			
					2000
0–1700	**Hittites Enter Anatolia**	***c.* 1900**			
	Assyrian traders at Kultepe	1900			
er 1700					BRONZE AGE
c. 1750					
0–1500	Mursilis I	1620–1590			
er 1500	**Rise of Mitanni**	***c.* 1500**			
er 1500	Phoenicians develop alphabet	*c.* 1500			
	Hittite Empire	**1400–1200**			
1400?					
0–1200	Suppiluliumas I	1380–1340			
	Battle of Kadesh	1300			
	Collapse of Hittites	1200			
1200	**Phrygian Occupation of Anatolia**	**1200–700**			1250
c. 1200	Invasions of Sea Peoples	*c.* 1200			
	Hebrews invade Canaan	*c.* 1200			
***c.* 1150**					
1100	Neo-Hittite kingdoms in northern Syria	after 1100			1000
	Rise of Sidon and Tyre	*c.* 1000	**Villanovan Culture in Italy**	**1000**	
	Assyrians Dominate Levant	**875–630**	**Height of Etruscan Civilization**	**800–500**	IRON AGE
775?	Phoenicians found Carthage	814?	Founding of Rome	753	
2–479	**Persian Conquest of Anatolia and Levant**	**540–538**	Rome expels Tarquins	510	
c. 450			**Decline of Etruscans**	**400–200**	
c. 330			Gauls invade Italy	400–300	
			Rome conquers Veii	396	
					B.C.

1 Crete · The Island of Minos

Europa was the daughter of Agenor, the king of Tyre. She was so beautiful that Zeus himself, the king of gods, fell in love with her. Europa and her companions were used to stroll near the sea-shore at Tyre, where Agenor's herds of cattle grazed. Zeus assumed the shape of a snow-white bull and mingled with them. Seeing the beautiful beast, Europa caressed it, whereupon Zeus contrived to get her on his back and swam with her across the sea to the far-off island of Crete. There he assumed the shape of an eagle and lay with the girl; the resultant offspring were Sarpedon, Rhadamanthus, and Minos, who became king of Crete.

Aegeus was king of Athens. He had a son, Theseus, by the daughter of Pittheus, king of Troezen, in whose palace the boy was brought up. When he grew to manhood Theseus went to Athens in search of his father. Medea, wife of Aegeus, tried to poison the young man before his father could recognize him, but she failed. Later Theseus, already renowned for many feats of heroism, volunteered to sail to Crete as one of the seven

Horns of consecration surmounting the palace of Minos; they probably represented the horns of sacrificed bulls.

youths who, with seven maidens, were sent every ninth year by Athens as tribute to King Minos.

In the labyrinth of his palace, Minos kept a monster, part bull and part man, the progeny of his wife, Pasiphaë, whom the sea god Poseidon had caused to be enamoured of a bull. Until Theseus arrived the fourteen youths and maidens were invariably devoured by the monster. Ariadne, the daughter of Minos, fell in love with the handsome Athenian, and gave him a ball of thread which he played out behind him as he penetrated the labyrinth. When he met the Minotaur in the dim depths, Theseus slew him 'by smiting him with his fists', and then, by following the thread, found his way out and into the arms of Ariadne. The two lovers fled to the island of Naxos, where Theseus deserted Ariadne. On his return to Athens he forgot to hoist the white sails that were the pre-arranged signal of his success in Crete. The stricken King Aegeus saw the ship's black sails – the signal that Theseus had lost in his encounter with the unnatural beast – threw himself into the sea, and drowned. Ever since it has been called the Aegean. So Theseus, in his turn, became the king of the Athenians.

The Greeks of the classical age believed these two familiar Greek myths. The Romans probably had doubts, and every succeeding age down to this one has regarded them as legends and nothing more. But nowadays we hardly know where we are. Historians, linguists, and practical-minded archaeologists comb the myths, the works of Homer, Hesiod, and other Greek poets in search of clues to archaeological sites. No one raises an eyebrow if a philologist like Leonard Palmer or an archaeologist such as Carl Blegen mingles his linguistic researches or excavation reports with references to what Homer said about King Nestor of Pylos or King Priam of Troy. This was not always so. In 1846 the monumental history of Greece by George Grote contained these words:

I begin the real history of Greece with the first recorded Olympiad, or 776 B.C. . . . For the truth is, that historical records, properly so called, do not begin until long after this date: nor will any man who candidly considers the extreme paucity of attested facts for two centuries after 776 B.C. be astonished to learn that the state of Greece in 900, 1000, 1100, 1200, 1300, 1400 B.C. – or any earlier century which it may please chronologists to include in their computed genealogies – cannot be described to him upon anything like decent evidence.

These earlier times, Grote observed in his writings, belong to the region of

epic poetry and legend. To confound together these disparate matters is, in my judgement, essentially unphilosophical.

What has happened to alter this view so radically? The answer is simply the development of scientific archaeology. We have seen how a number of Old Testament records relating to ancient Egypt and Mesopotamia have been confirmed. But there was more gratification than surprise when the religious chronicles of the Hebrews were corroborated by archaeological discoveries. It *was* surprising, however, to find not only Homer's story of the Trojan War, but even the most fantastic myths and legends partially confirmed by the evidence of the spade. But the matter is much more complex than whether or not such and such a legend described actual beings, circumstances, and events. The modern archaeologist does not believe in the literal reality of Poseidon or the Minotaur or Europa any more than Grote did. But at the same time it is no longer possible to take refuge in the idea that these myths express mere poetic or symbolic truths. The reality lies somewhere in between, for now the myths have been proved to contain elements of historical truth.

To make matters more difficult, the story is still unfolding, the pattern changing, even as these words are being written. No sooner does one think one has found a way out of the labyrinth than some scholar shouts, 'No! Not that way – it's a blind alley.' And so we go on groping – but with what zest!

The area with which we are here concerned comprises Crete, the Aegean Islands, the mainland of Greece, and western Asia Minor. As we have seen, by about 2800 B.C. two major civilizations had developed, one in Africa and the other in the Near East. (A few centuries later a third civilization emerged in the Indus Valley, much farther to the east, but that does not enter into this picture.) Egypt was already in trading contact with the coast of Lebanon and Palestine in predynastic times. During the Old Kingdom she established colonies there, and was

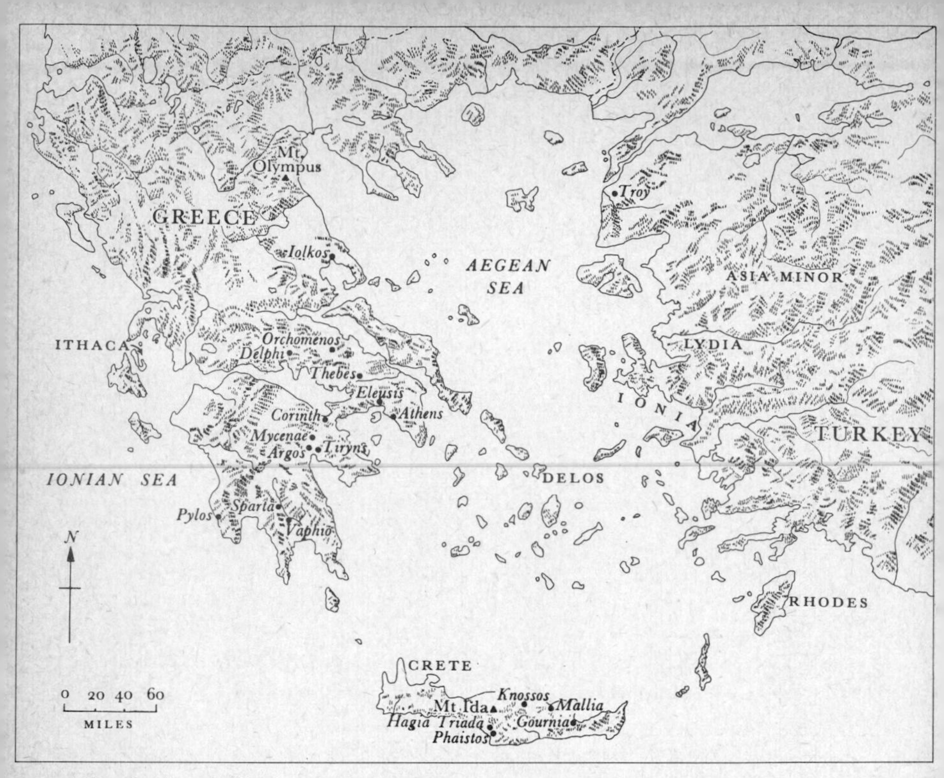

Bronze Age civilizations in the Aegean.

trading also with the Aegean Islands. A glance at the map will show that there is a chain of islands linking Greece with the Turkish mainland; the southernmost of these is the long, narrow, mountainous island of Crete. South of Crete there is nothing but sea until one reaches the African coast; not a wide stretch by modern standards, but in days when ships rarely sailed out of sight of a coast, sufficient to make Crete fairly remote from Egypt, which at that time was the nearest civilized power.

During the nineteenth century, archaeologists had devoted most of their attention not to the islands of the Aegean, but to the mainland. Between 1870 and 1884 the brilliant, eccentric German amateur archaeologist, Heinrich Schliemann, had excavated at Troy, near the Hellespont, and at Mycenae, Tiryns, and Orchomenos in Greece. He believed that the Trojan War was not legendary, but a historical event, and he confounded the sceptics by discovering remains of buildings, and arms, ornaments, and other works of bronze, gold, and ivory, some of which closely resembled objects described in the *Iliad* and the *Odyssey*. These finds – which included daggers of gold-inlaid bronze; gold diadems, dress ornaments, and rings; gold drinking vessels, offering vases (rhytons), and cult objects – were of a type not previously found in Europe. The art was exquisite – sensitive, vigorous, yet disciplined, the goldwork being especially fine. About ninety years ago, when these treasures were first discovered, precise archaeological dating did not exist. No one knew exactly how old Schliemann's finds were, but in his enthusiasm he confidently attributed them to the period of the Trojan War, traditionally dated about 1190 B.C., although it is now placed somewhat earlier by a good many important scholars.

But there were other scholars who were not so easily satisfied, and controversy waxed bitter during the twenty years following the initial discoveries at Troy. One critic attributed the goldwork of Mycenae to the Byzantine period. Others, including the English scholar Arthur Evans, believed that it was older than the period of the Trojan War. Meanwhile all such artifacts, wherever found, were labelled Mycenaean, from the name of the type-site. Evans (who was later knighted) met Schliemann in 1883 in Athens and spent much time examining the Mycenaean treasures. The Englishman had a sensitive, almost intuitive understanding of the changes and developments of artistic style; Mycenaean art fascinated and intrigued him. Handling the gold cups and the diadems, jewels, and intaglios in Schliemann's great villa, Evans wondered who could possibly have produced such art. It had been found in Greece, yet there was little in it of the classical Greek spirit. But it was not Oriental either. Evans was excited and puzzled by what he considered possible Near Eastern influences. He politely listened when the old German pointed out enthusiastically the resemblances between the twin-handled cup with its feeding doves that he had discovered at Mycenae and the Cup of Nestor described by Homer. But he was more interested in the problem of Mycenaean origins than he was in tracing connexions with Homer. Objects of such beauty and craftsmanship must be the products of a long period of civilization. The evidence uncovered by Schliemann obviously indicated a pre-Greek culture along and about the Aegean coast. Might it not have been literate, as Egypt's was? Evans had almost microscopic eyesight when viewing things at close range. The conviction grew on him that the tiny marks on some of the smaller objects might be pictographs, elements of a hitherto unknown language.

Evans's eye for very small, significant detail had been helpful to him in his study of numismatics, though this was only one of his many interests. He was an extremely complex character, well-read in many fields – especially ancient history and prehistory – sensitive to art and beauty, yet no mere aesthete or academician, but a vigorous man of action. Before meeting Schliemann in 1883 he had travelled widely in Sweden, Finland, and the Balkan countries which he most loved. When Bosnia and Herzegovina revolted against their Turkish oppressors, Evans championed them enthusiastically, became a war correspondent for the *Manchester Guardian*, and eventually was arrested as a spy and expelled. And yet throughout all these political and journalistic activities he found time to follow his archaeological bent – copying inscriptions or collecting coins and other antiquities – when he was not swimming a swollen river naked (except for a hat into which his notebook was tucked), or entering a Moslem stronghold wearing his red-lined cloak inside out and trying to look as Oriental as possible. The year after his meeting with Schliemann, Evans, at the age of thirty-three, was appointed Keeper of the Ashmolean Museum at Oxford, in which academic post he succeeded in consolidating the scattered archaeological material at Oxford into a central museum of art and archaeology. This accomplished, he found considerable time for foreign travel once again.

These personal details are extremely relevant to the story of Evans's discoveries. His forceful, positive character imprinted itself on whatever he did. The storm of debate that still rumbles around the conclusions he drew from his archaeological discoveries and studies is proof of this. Twenty-one years after his death he remains a figure of controversy.

During the fifteen years following his success at Oxford he made several trips to Greece and Sicily, at intervals in his museum work. The question whether prehistoric Greece had a writing system that had long been lost was never far from his mind. In 1893 he was in Athens with John Myres (later Sir John) – that 'black-bearded Ulysses' – with whom he spent time 'grubbing ... below the "Pelasgian" wall of the Acropolis and picking out fragments of pre-Mycenaean vases which nobody here seems to have heeded before', to quote from one of his letters. And he studied Mycenaean rings. One day Evans was searching among the trays of the antiquity dealers in Shoe Lane in Athens when he came upon several tiny bead seals, some four-sided, some three-sided, drilled with a hole for thread. Scrutinizing them with his remarkable eyesight, Evans thought again that he could detect 'squiggles' that might be writing symbols.

He asked the dealer where they came from and was told that they were from Crete. The seals were called *galopetres* – 'milk stones' – because the peasant women there wore them around their necks as charms when they suckled their children. Subsequently, in Crete, he could not persuade a nursing mother to sell her 'milk stone'; to have parted from it, she believed, would have imperilled her child's health.

The year 1893 was a critical one in Evans's life. In that year his much-loved wife, Margaret, died after a long illness. Partly to distract his mind from this tragedy, but largely because he felt he had found an important clue to his mystery, he decided to go to Crete. Almost from the moment he set foot on Cretan soil Evans fell in love with the island, as so many travellers have done since. He loved the mountainous landscape, with snow-crowned Mount Ida, where Zeus himself had been born, and Mount Juktas, where lay the legendary tomb of the god. With a guide he explored the island on foot and on muleback. Not only did he find many more 'milk stones', but potsherds, gems, and, among other things, remains of prehistoric settlements. Evans had come to Europa's island. Here, as Homer had written, was

a rich and lovely land, washed by the waves on every side . . . and boasting ninety cities. . . . One of the ninety towns is a great city called

Knossos, and there ... King Minos ruled and enjoyed the friendship of almighty Zeus.

Knossos – a mere village now – still existed, a few miles from the port of Herakleion. Schliemann, of course, had also been well aware of Homeric allusions to this and other places on the island, and had planned to dig at Knossos, but a hitch in negotiations over the land had been followed not long after by his death. Evans's interest in things Homeric was at that time only peripheral. His main concern was to find further evidence of a writing system. At Knossos there was a large, flat-topped mound where a Cretan investigator (appropriately named Minos) had already dug and found remains of massive walls and many huge pithoi, or storage jars. Another Mycenaean palace, perhaps? It was enough to make up Evans's mind. If there was a palace there might be archives, like those discovered at Assurbanipal's palace at Nineveh.

After Crete was freed from Turkish rule in 1899, it became possible for Evans, with the help of the Commissioner of Crete, Prince George of Greece, to secure a share of the site for archaeological exploration. In March 1900 he returned to the island and was joined by two companions, D. G. Hogarth and Duncan Mackenzie, both experienced archaeologists. He arrived in the midst of a great storm; thunder pealed from the crags of the mountain where the god of lightning had been born. After this singularly dramatic introduction Evans began digging, and almost at once he uncovered a great labyrinth of buildings.

He soon found the palace store-rooms – the great stone-built magazines with their rows of smoke-blackened pithoi, more than man-high, that had once contained olive oil, wine, honey, figs, and other products of the island. And not far away Evans came upon what he had been looking for: the first hoard of clay tablets, inscribed with symbols – not Egyptian hieroglyphs, not Sumerian cuneiform, but a script he remembered having seen on another such tablet that had come from Knossos.

Even before he began digging Evans had written:

The great days of Crete were those of which we still find a reflection in the Homeric poems – the period of Mycenaean culture, to which here at least we would fain attach the name 'Minoan' [after King Minos of the Greek legend]. ... Nothing more continually strikes the archaeological explorer of its ancient remains than the comparative paucity and unimportance of the relics of the historical period. ... The golden age of Crete lies far beyond the limits of [that] period. ...

But only a month after the start of his excavations he could write in his diary:

The extraordinary phenomenon: nothing Greek – nothing Roman. . . . Even geometrical [Greek pottery of the pre-classical period] fails us – though as tholoi found near [the] central road show, a flourishing Knossos existed lower down. . . . Nay, its great period goes at least well back to the pre-Mycenaean period.

At the age of forty-eight Evans had found his destiny, which was to devote the rest of his life to excavating and interpreting Knossos. The gods of Crete had claimed him, and, like Theseus, his task was to penetrate the Minoan labyrinth.

Evans was right in his intuition; the civilization that had flourished in Crete was extremely ancient. When the development of sequence dating by pottery styles and by stratification enabled archaeologists to affix reasonably accurate dates to objects, it became evident that the oldest shaft graves that Schliemann had found at Mycenae did not date earlier than 1600 B.C. At Knossos, however, Evans was able to trace a sequence of almost continuous development from about 3000 B.C. down to about 1150 B.C. Yet from the beginnings of this Minoan civilization (Evans's name for it has stuck) the style of pottery, fresco painting, arms, and ornaments resembled the type that had been previously called Mycenaean. So-called Mycenaean objects appeared to be only a late development of this style, and one plausible inference was that mainland sites such as Mycenae were Minoan colonies. This is what Evans believed, but as we shall see, the facts are considerably more complex.

Evans devoted thirty years and, even though he was helped for a while by the Cretan Exploration Fund, a considerable part of his personal fortune to the excavation and restoration of the Knossian palace. Although he early recognized that the clay tablets were lists or inventories of some sort, he never succeeded in deciphering them; but his interest in the Minoan writing system remained undiminished.

Lacking intelligible written documents, apart from legends and traditions recorded by later poets and historians, Evans and other early workers in Cretan archaeology had to rely on material evidence for their interpretation of Minoan civilization. Evans's monumental work of scholarship, *The Palace of Minos*, is, with the restored palace, a permanent memorial at once to his genius and to his firmly held beliefs. But numerous other gifted scholars have helped to unravel the mystery, and not all have agreed entirely with Evans's conclusions. Federigo Halbherr, the distinguished Italian archaeologist, worked for many years in the south with an expedition at the great palace of Phaistos and at Hagia Triada, having in fact preceded Evans in other parts of Crete. Harriet Boyd Hawes worked at Gournia and Richard Seager at other sites in the east. R. C. Bosanquet and R. M. Dawkins and colleagues dug at Praisos and Palaikastro. French scholars unearthed another Minoan palace at Mallia. Spyridon Marinatos and other Greek archaeologists have made distinguished contributions, both in excavation and interpretation. Again, on the Greek mainland the work of Alan Wace and John Papadimitriou at Mycenae and Carl Blegen at Pylos have cast fresh light on the later period of Aegean civilization. These and a number of other significant contributions have indeed caused a drastic revision of earlier opinions.

The efforts of these men and women have enabled us to draw an impressive, though still incomplete, picture of Europe's earliest civilization. But for the full impact of the initial discoveries as they were revealed year after year, we have to turn to Evans. During the first few years of his excavations at Knossos he made discoveries that astonished the archaeological world. He revealed that the palace, built around a large central courtyard on top of a mound called Kephala, was truly labyrinthine in its complexity. About the Central Court, which one approached via one or another of several long corridors, was a veritable maze of halls, private chambers, store-rooms, staircases, ramps, and other areas to serve special purposes. And on one of the plastered interior walls Evans came upon the first

The queen's apartments, Knossos.

representation of a Minoan man to have been discovered. It was a painted fresco, in a fragmentary condition, but sufficient to recall to Evans a painting that had been found in the tomb of the Egyptian vizier Rekhmire at Thebes.

Rekhmire, chief minister under Pharaoh Tuthmosis III (1504–1450 B.C.), had had depicted on the walls of his tomb the reception of certain visiting foreigners, referred to as the *Keftiu*. They were completely non-Egyptian both in physique and in dress: very thin-waisted, elegant, with their dark,

Bull's-head rhyton discovered in a cult centre of the palace complex at Knossos. It was probably used for libations, which were poured into it through a hole at the top of the neck, and trickled out through an opening in the mouth.

curled hair worn in a side-lock, or sometimes two locks, falling over one shoulder, and attired in short kilts. Similar figures appear in other Egyptian wall paintings. In some instances the 'gifts' they carried to present to the Egyptians resembled in style objects discovered by Schliemann at Mycenae. One of the figures, indeed, carried a rhyton in the form of a bull's head, almost exactly like the rhyton found in one of the shaft graves.

The fresco that Evans's workmen uncovered included a figure of just this kind, slightly larger than life-size, and with details that were missing from the Egyptian artists' paintings. To Evans the head was not classically Greek, but recalled an indigenous Cretan type. The body, though firm and muscular, nevertheless was slim and suggested a delicate refinement. The skin was a kind of russet-brown, the kilt was orange with a blue band near the base, the hands carried a tall rhyton, painted blue to indicate, by convention, that it represented silver – all similar to those shown in the Egyptian paintings. The figure had been one in a procession of similar figures painted on the walls of the corridor. Here then was one of the mysterious *Keftiu* who had traded with Egypt in the fifteenth century B.C.

From the west side of the Central Court opened a number of rooms, the most dramatic of which was the Throne Room. It was a comparatively small, rectangular chamber, divided on one side from a second room of about the same size by a balustrade surmounted by columns. The floor of this second room was at a lower level, forming a kind of pit. Evans thought at first it might be a bath, but later concluded that it was a lustral basin, probably used for ceremonial purposes. Against the wall facing the basin stood a thirty-four-hundred-year-old alabaster throne, the oldest in Europe. Flanked by stone benches that ran along the wall, it was rather like the bishop's throne in the chapter house of a medieval cathedral. Fragmented wall frescoes showed that on each side of the throne had been painted pictures of griffins and conventionalized foliage. Near by on the floor lay vessels, evidently used in some kind of religious ceremony, but they had been overturned and were in disorder.

West of this room, and separated from it by a corridor, lay the long, rectangular magazines that contained the huge

The throne room in the palace of Minos. (The frescoes are modern replicas.)

pithoi: these, clearly, were the palace store-rooms, the repositories of Minos' wealth – olive oil, wine, cereals, fruits; in the floors were sunk cists or 'safe deposits' which may have contained gold and other treasure similar to that which Schliemann had found in the graves at Mycenae. (As in ancient Egypt, wealth was in kind, not in currency.) At the end of one corridor was found a complex of smaller rooms, the offices of the scribes and clerks, who had kept records of this wealth on clay tablets in a script that Evans could not read. And there were not only offices, but other rooms which had clearly been the workshops of craftsmen and artisans – metalworkers, potters, stone carvers, and so forth. In one such chamber the excavators found a block of stone half sawed through, as if abandoned suddenly by the craftsman.

In many places were the marks of fire, particularly in the magazines, where some of the pithoi were blackened by the smoke of the oil that they had once contained and that had burned. By noting the direction of these smoke stains, it was even possible to establish that the wind was blowing from the south on the day that fire destroyed Knossos. The palace must have burned fiercely, because there was much wood in its construction. The walls had been reinforced with timber supports; the pillars, which tapered from capital to base, were also hewn out of timber, and Evans found the charred remains of the columns in their original stone bases.

Still farther north, on the side of the palace facing the sea, the excavators came upon a monumental gateway, the Northern Entrance or Sea Gate. This too had been magnificent in its time, with an ascending stone-paved road passing between porticoes with downward-tapering columns and leading to the Central Court. But what was most remarkable was that on the pavement beneath one of the portico walls overlooking the passage were found fragments of a vivid painted plaster relief of a charging bull. By this time Evans and his collaborators, though more methodical and scientific than Schliemann had been, began partly to share the German amateur's respect for the ancient myths. The story of Theseus, Ariadne, and the Minotaur had begun to loom large in their minds; the image of a bull had recurred in fact and fable. There was the bull's-head rhyton found at Mycenae, and the story of Europa who had been carried to Crete by Zeus in the shape of a bull. One encountered the creature again and again.

Evans was a romantic, though a scholar, but it is doubtful whether he or any of the various archaeologists, architects, and other specialists who from time to time worked with him were given to fantasy. They were looking for facts, not trying to justify an earlier formed hypothesis, as Schliemann had tried to do. But the facts were there before their eyes. Not only did they discover the famous relief of the charging bull, but other frescoes that brought them much nearer to the legend of Theseus and Ariadne. One of these depicts another charging bull, but this time it is not alone. There are three human figures, two female and one male. The girls (identifiable by their lighter skins, by a convention similar to that applied in Egypt) stand at each end of the painting. In the centre of the picture a male athlete (wearing, like the girls, only a loincloth) is in the act of somersaulting over the bull's back.

The seven youths and seven maidens sent from Athens to be sacrificed to the bull-monster – the labyrinth – Theseus and Ariadne – Pasiphaë, wife of Minos, who fell in love with a bull – were these, after all, mere poetic fantasies? They had appeared to be, and yet here was a picture of a young man and two young women performing a feat that recalled the ancient myth, a feat so difficult that it seemed impossible. If this were a true record of fact, then perhaps it might be proved that the legends themselves were not completely implausible. One may imagine the discussions and arguments that went on between Evans and his colleagues in the Villa Ariadne, the house that he had built near the palace. In an attempt to reconstruct how the bull-leaping trick might have been done, Evans suggested that each athlete in turn grasped the animal's horns, vaulted in a somersault over its head, landed upright on its back, and then leaped off over its tail, probably in another somersault, into the arms of a waiting companion. A cow-puncher from Arizona who was consulted thought this was quite inconceivable, however, since a charging bull lowers its horns and twists its head sideways. Anyone rash enough to attempt to grasp the horns, he claimed, would undoubtedly be gored and tossed aside.

The excavators of Knossos discovered another related fresco, which depicts a large number of men and women seated or standing in a kind of grandstand and evidently watching some public performance. The women are apparently court ladies in full coiffure of curled hair beset with jewels. Their puffed

'La Parisienne.' The knot at the back of her neck may be merely a fashionable detail of dress, or it may be a sign that she was a priestess, for sacral knots were a common religious symbol.

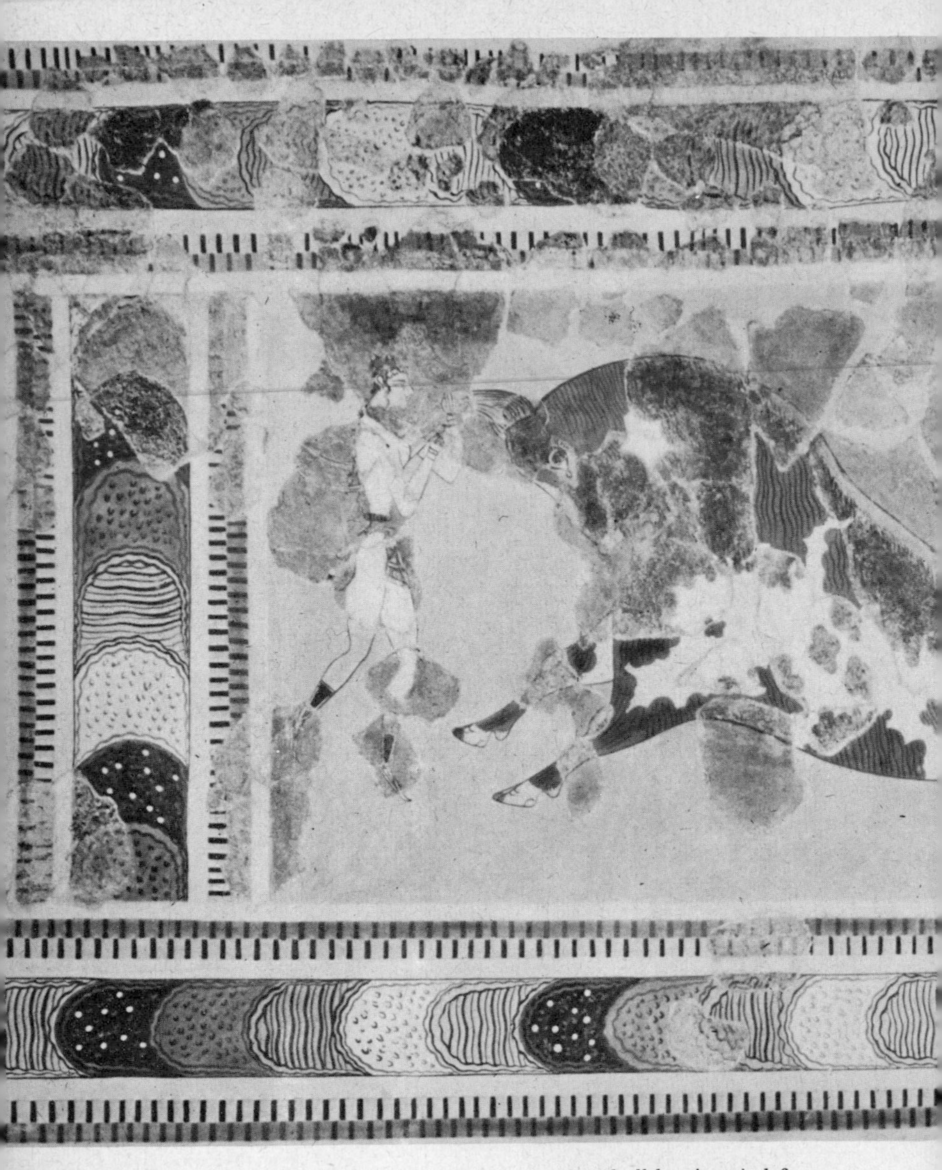

A fresco from the palace at Knossos shows acrobats bull-leaping. At left, a girl puts her arm around the horn of the bull so that he will lift his head in anger and attempt to toss her. With the aid of this momentum, she will

somersault over his back, as another acrobat can be seen doing. The girl standing behind the bull is poised ready to catch the leapers and steady them as they reach the ground.

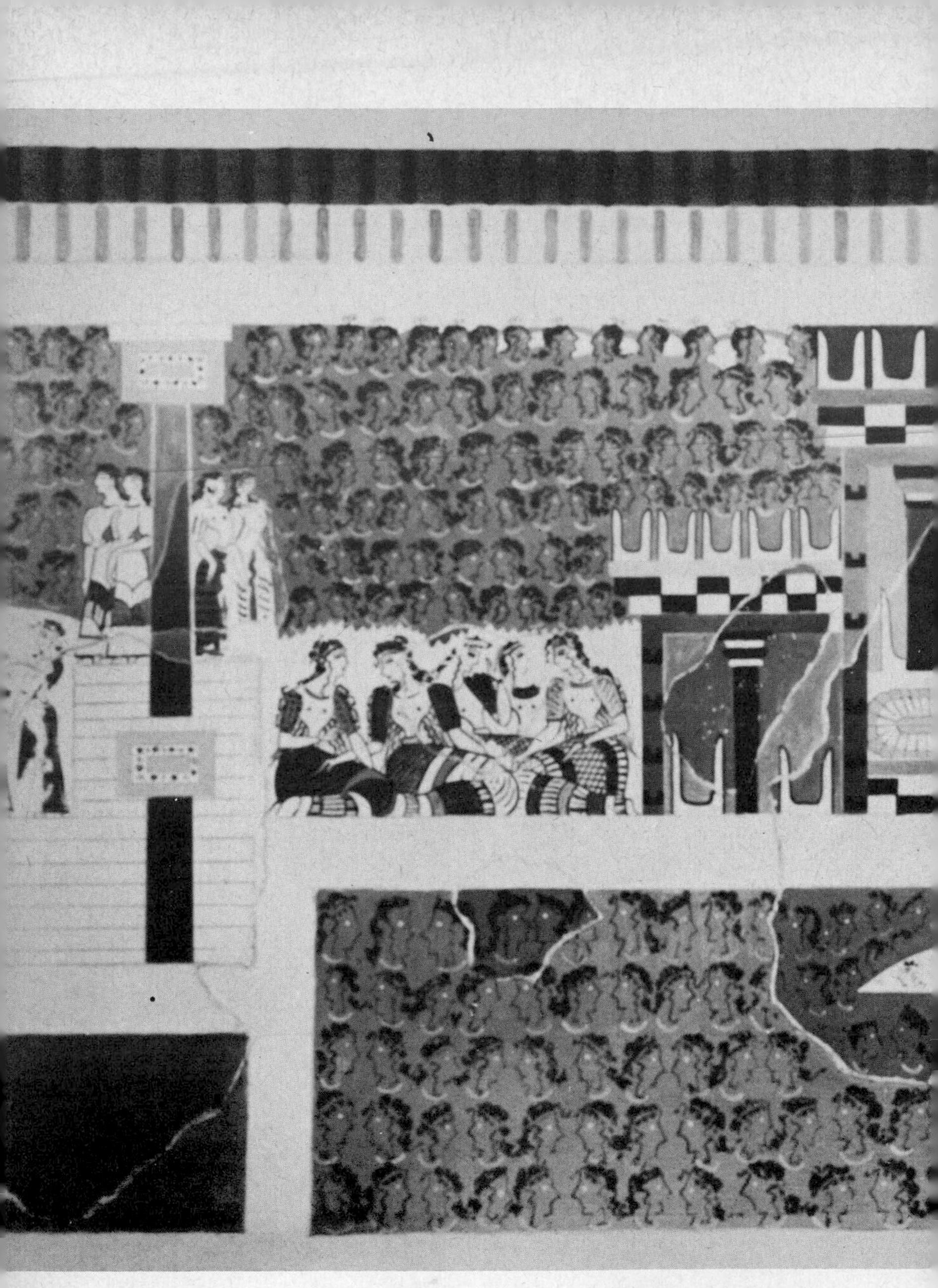

An audience watched a ceremonial dance or a bull-leaping performance. The shrine at the centre is marked by horns of consecration. The artist has

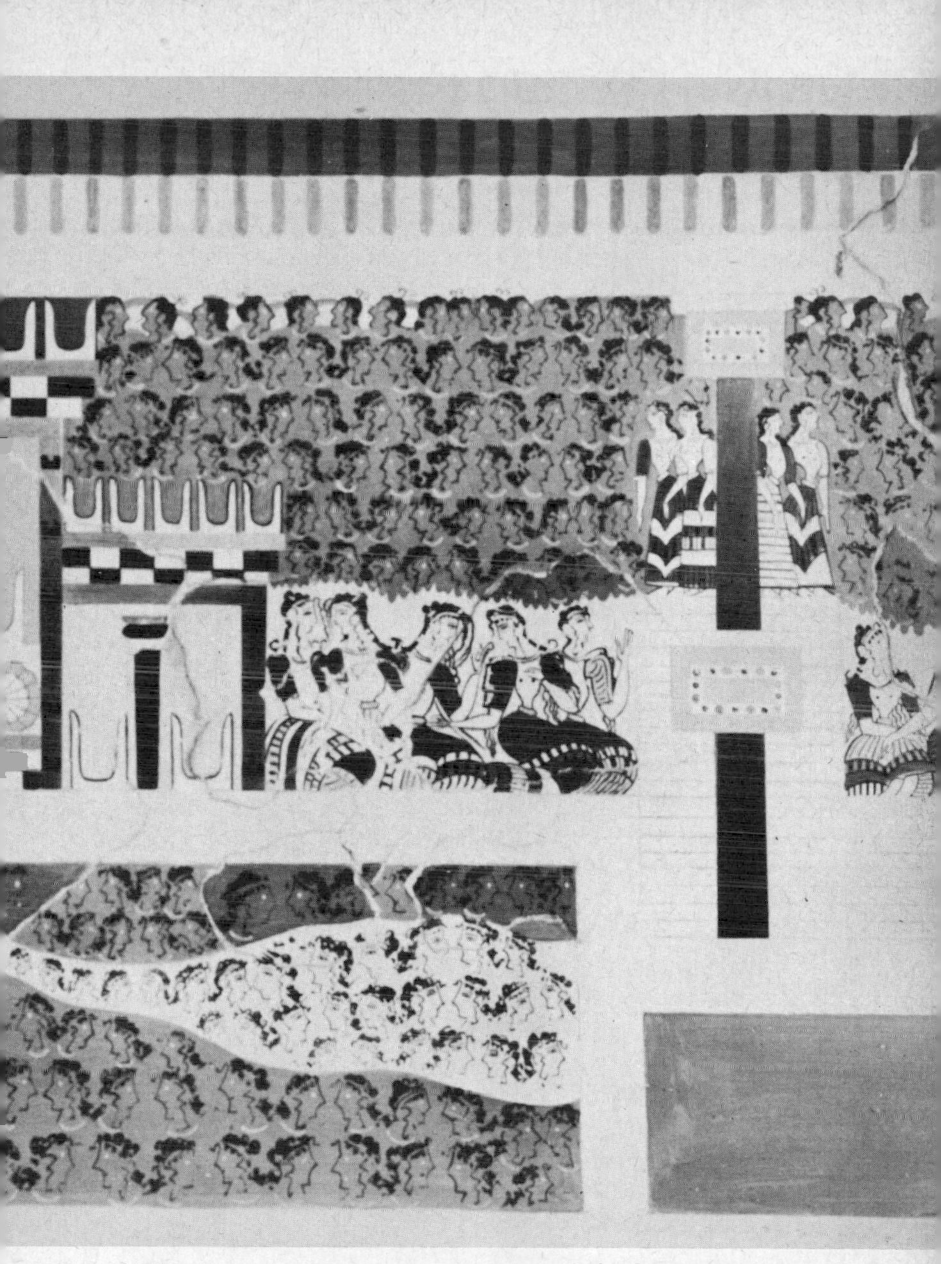

depicted most of the audience with a few impressionistic strokes and devoted careful attention to drawing the colourfully dressed court ladies.

sleeves, their flounced, bell-shaped skirts, and their general air of sophistication made a French visitor to the site in the early nineteen-hundreds exclaim, 'Why, they are *Parisiennes*!'

But their breasts are bared and even the *Parisiennes* of the early twentieth century would hardly have dared to appear at the Opéra in such full décolletage. In any event these Minoan ladies, gossiping and chatting as they wait for the ceremony to begin, do not seem to be self-conscious. To all intents they might be chic women at a party who are waiting for something exciting to happen. In the same fresco are depicted hundreds of male spectators, mere caricatures indicated by only a few strokes of the draughtsman's hand, crowded into the grandstand almost as if to fill up space. It is hardly an exaggeration to say that this scene could have been sketched by a talented newspaper illustrator to adorn a gossip column. What are these rows of *soignée* women and girls and the men behind them waiting for or looking at?

It is possible that they were anticipating, or watching, the performance shown in the other fresco, and that this was part of a religious ceremony or ritual. In the centre of the audience scene there is what appears to be a shrine, with downward-tapering pillars and conventionalized representations of the horns of a bull – the 'horns of consecration', to use Evans's phrase – a motif that appears frequently in the decoration of Minoan palaces and on seals and pottery. There can be no doubt that the bull-leaping sport was in some way associated with the observance of religious practices.

For what presiding deity was this shrine intended? Although the Cretans of later times boasted that their island was both the birthplace and burial place of Zeus, king of the gods, there is little evidence in Minoan art of a prominent male deity. Admittedly men appear in religious or cult scenes, but always in subordinate positions. The principal deity is always a goddess. As in other eastern religions, the male god associated with her may have been her son or her lover; and as in such other religions he may have been ritually sacrificed each year. But the goddess reigned eternally. One sees her in delicately modelled, slim-waisted figurines, with belled or flounced ankle-length skirts. Sometimes her back and upper arms are covered.

Scene engraved upon a gold ring showing a group of female worshippers in flounced skirts, dancing in a field of lilies to evoke the mother goddess.

She also appears frequently on Minoan and Mycenaean seals, rings, and gems, usually alone, but sometimes accompanied by male or female figures, and very often near a sacred tree or grove. Occasionally an altar is shown, before which women, dressed like the goddess in flounced skirts, are dancing. One of the most fascinating of the seals depicts two rampant lions supporting a central pillar – recalling the Lion Gate at Mycenae, but here the pillar is crowned by a goddess. In some frescoes the women appear to be wearing puffed sleeves on to which their dark hair falls in ringlets; but always the breasts are bare, and on some of the intaglios the goddess is naked to the waist.

In the Central Sanctuary of the palace at Knossos the excavators discovered what had evidently been the shrine of a goddess, and here they found an exquisite little statuette in faience. It represents a woman whose whole body is clothed save for her face, forearms, and bosom. In each outstretched hand she grasps a writhing snake, and on her head is a circular head-dress adorned with the miniature figure of a leopard. Her bodice is so tight that it forces the breasts into unnatural prominence, and below the wasp-like waist an elegant skirt falls in pleated flounces to her feet. Among primitive peoples, even today, the snake is frequently associated with the earth and with earth worship, and for that reason it is equally apt to call this obviously hieratic figure either the snake goddess or the earth goddess.

In ancient religions in which sexual and fertility symbols are prominent, the archetypal figure of the mother goddess, or the earth mother, is almost universal. One finds her in palaeolithic times, usually represented as a crude figure with enormous breasts, big buttocks, and a swollen belly. In the Near East she survived long into historical times as Diana of Ephesus, or in more shapely aspects as Ishtar. In Minoan Crete she became sophisticated, even elegant. When the smart ladies of the court of Knossos exposed their bosoms in public, as shown in the palace frescoes, it would seem they followed a custom amply sanctioned by old religious traditions.

In various aspects, the mother goddess survived in the religion of classical Greece. Demeter represented her as the earth mother who nourished mankind and increased the fertility of the fields. Aphrodite continued her role as the goddess of love. Athena was the goddess as warrior, and Artemis, the chaste huntress, inherited her power over the wild beasts. (Minoan representations frequently show the mother goddess taming lions and bulls, or fabulous animals such as griffins and sphinxes.) The Central Sanctuary, where the goddess's image was discovered, was not the only area of the Knossos palace dedicated to her. The whole palace was sacred in character, a fact that has given support to the theory that the sacral role of the Cretan princes was as important to the country as their secular functions were.

The living quarters and the state rooms of the palace, approached by the Grand Staircase, lay in the south-east wing of the structure and were built at various levels above and below that of the Central Court, into the steep hillside that falls away towards the river Kairatos. This wing, by far the most

The snake goddess.

impressive remaining part of the great building, owes its present dignity and splendour as much to Evans's painstaking restoration and reconstruction as to the efforts of the original architects. As the palace fell into ruin this section suffered less than the others. By the time the wooden columns supporting the Grand Staircase and the state rooms collapsed or decayed, the debris from the roof and the upper walls had formed a compact filling, resting on the lower parts of the building and serving as a continued support for much of the remains of the staircase and the upper structure.

Through this deposit of fifteen hundred years Greek miners engaged by Evans tunnelled their way, shoring up walls and roofs. Meanwhile the resident architect, Christian Doll, carefully examined and made plans of the remains. Here were the bases on which the wooden pillars had once rested; there, on parts of the walls that were still standing, were fragments of plaster with painted scenes still adhering to them. Bit by bit, with infinite care and patience, Evans and his colleagues restored the staircase and the rooms to which it led.

The result is awe-inspiring. Admittedly, to visit unrestored Phaistos with its ruined walls and staircases open to the sky and with snow-capped Mount Ida in the distance is a moving experience. In a different way, so is it to see Mallia, Gournia, and other open sites. But the very openness of their ruins, bathed in sunlight, gives a false impression of what a Minoan palace was like. Whereas when one descends that shadowed Knossian staircase, with its colonnades opening on to a light-well, or when one stands in the dimly lit, frescoed rooms of state, one feels nearest to those remote people whose character has been aptly described as 'a curious mixture of religious formalism and a real *joie de vivre* of a somewhat heartless and childlike nature'.

Evans himself felt this strongly. In a memorable passage from *The Palace of Minos* he wrote:

During an attack of fever, having found, for the sake of better air, a temporary lodging in the room below the inspection tower that has been erected on the neighbouring edge of the Central Court, and tempted in the warm moonlight to look down the staircase-well, the whole place seemed to awake awhile to life and movement. Such was

The 'Priest-King'.

the force of the illusion that the Priest-King with his plumed lily crown, great ladies, tightly girdled, flounced, and corseted, long-stoled priests, and after them a retinue of elegant but sinewy youths – as if the Cup-Bearer and his fellows had stepped down from the walls – passed and repassed on the flights below.

At Knossos and other Minoan sites archaeologists have come upon pillars, often set in or beside small stone-lined basins let into the floor of a room and inscribed with the sign of the *labrys*, or double axe. Many actual examples of such axes in bronze and other metals have come to light, some of them, no doubt, strictly functional objects. But the form, sometimes set on a base or between the horns of consecration, also appears in materials and sizes unsuitable for any practical purpose. It was

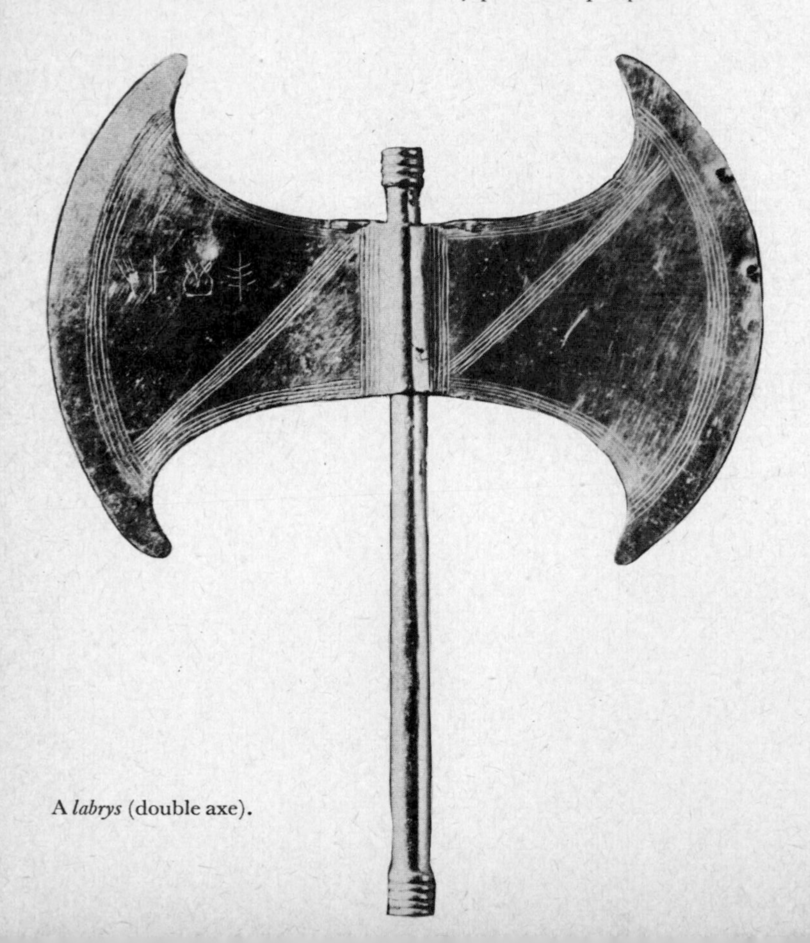

A *labrys* (double axe).

clearly a sacred symbol. Evans and other scholars have suggested that it might have been associated with some rite intended to propitiate the infernal powers, a theory supported by the fact that Crete is subject to earthquakes, some of which have been catastrophic.

Because he found such symbols on its walls, Evans called one of the state rooms of the Knossos palace the Hall of the Double Axes. By means of double doors that swung on rectangular pillars, the inner area of this hall could be closed off – on the one side from an area with two porticoes facing spacious light-wells, and on the other from what Evans referred to as an audience chamber, since here he found evidence of a canopied throne. Painted on a spiraliform frieze on the walls of another near-by room – the Hall of the Colonnades – Evans had found representations of the huge leather figure-of-eight shields so often encountered in Minoan – and Mycenaean – art. On the upper walls of the Hall of the Double Axes he found traces of the same frieze, but no shields. Evans conjectured that real shields once hung there, and had replicas made. For this and other touches of disciplined, if bold, imagination he has been criticized by men with a more cautious approach to archaeology.

Not far from this hall, but approachable only via a dark, winding corridor, is another suite of rooms, the largest room of which Evans called the Queen's Megaron. There is no certain proof that these were indeed the queen's chambers, but their privacy and a certain femininity in the decoration strongly suggest it. Also they were linked by a private stairway with the quarters directly above. On one side, opposite the main door, a colonnade opens on to a light-well which softly illuminates the interior. Fragments of painted frescoes enabled Evans's artist, Édouard Gilliéron, to restore the main scheme of the delightful mural decoration. Dark blue dolphins sport on a light ground, against which one also sees smaller fish, sea plants, and other marine life of diverse colours. The walls and the ceiling are ornamented with the characteristic Minoan spirals and rosettes, and a dancing girl appears on one of the pillars.

One of the smaller adjoining rooms had an earthenware bath,

The dolphin fresco, Knossos (detail).

like a Victorian hip-bath, still *in situ*. Even more remarkable was the clear evidence, found in another small chamber, of a latrine. Evans wrote:

> The aperture leading to the main drain, partly masked by a curious projection, deviates from the centre of the seat, thus leaving room on the right for some vessel used for flushing the basin. As an anticipation of scientific methods of sanitation, the system of which we have here the record has been attained by few nations even at the present day.

At Knossos, Gournia, and Hagia Triada there is evidence of brilliant hydraulic engineering. Knossos in particular has been called a 'plumber's paradise'. Each area of the palace was served by a drainage system that fed into the main channel which, in turn, emptied into the river east of the hill. From the roof, rain-water was led through channels in the walls to underground drains ventilated by air shafts. Manholes gave admittance to these sewers, some of which were so large that Evans's excavators could spend whole days working in them without inconvenience. Two other features show the knowledge possessed by the Minoan engineers of more than thirty-five hundred years ago. In some cases water was taken through terracotta pipes with fitted sections that were tapered to produce a greater head of water and prevent accumulation of

Terracotta bathtub decorated with figures of cattle; such tubs were frequently provided with lids and used as sarcophagi as well.

sediment. In another instance an open channel was cut beside a steep flight of steps that leads from a bastion of the Central Court down to the river. Each flight of steps was at a right angle to the next; if the base of the channel had been smooth the water would have rushed down like a cataract and spilled over the sides. But the Minoan builders constructed the channel in a series of parabolic curves, of such a shape and size as to slow down the flow of water and enable it to take the right-angle turns without overspilling.

Though they varied in size and planning, other Minoan palaces and private villas were built in a manner generally similar to the great Knossian palace. All had stone walls reinforced by timber, tapering wooden columns, light-wells, large halls, and usually bathrooms and toilets. The palaces had open courtyards from which sprang a maze of rooms, corridors, and staircases; in a number of instances important rooms were covered with delicately painted frescoes in the general style of those we have already considered. On the ground floor there were frequently lustral basins and pillar rooms with one or more sacred pillars, often inscribed with representations of the double axe.

Again, in the other principal palaces at Phaistos and Mallia there were, as at Knossos, storage magazines, offices for clerks

Plaque, probably part of a miniature town scene inlaid on a chest.

and administrators, and workshops for numerous craftsmen. Knossos was by far the largest palace, covering some three acres and capable of housing several hundred people. These buildings were, in fact, not only royal or princely residences, but also cult centres, manufactories, arsenals, and administrative headquarters, all combined in one huge, multi-storeyed, multi-roomed structure.

But of course only the ruling families and their retinues lived in palaces. Around each palace are the remains of sizeable towns; the ruins at Knossos, which mark the site of one of the most ancient towns in Europe, are extensive enough to keep archaeologists busy for generations. There were also towns without such great palaces, and numerous luxurious private villas – some almost as large as the palaces – which stood alone on superb natural sites, as at Vathypetro, south of Knossos, and at Hagia Triada. There were ports and harbours and well-paved roads linking the various centres of population. Indeed, Crete was, Homer claimed, 'densely populated . . . boasting ninety cities'. Along the streets many of the houses were two or three storeys high, constructed of brick or stone, with windows on each storey. Each house probably had a roof terrace, which could also serve as a summer bedroom. A unique group of faience plaques, discovered at Knossos and representing a street scene, gives us a trustworthy idea of the appearance of Minoan cities.

In Cretan palaces and towns archaeologists have found exten-

Cup decorated with a band of roses and a knot of religious significance.

sive remains of workshops. The town at Gournia, for instance, seems to have been occupied almost entirely by craftsmen. Harriet Hawes, digging there some sixty years ago, came upon many small dwellings that had been both the homes and workshops of these artisans. In one house she found a whole carpenter's kit concealed in a cranny and, near by, the rotted remains of a wooden shelf that had supported fourteen loom weights arranged in order. One house contained a vat for refining olive oil still resting on its stone bench, with a place in front of it for an amphora into which the sediment could be poured. The products of such concentrated industry were certainly intended not only for home consumption but also for foreign trade.

Among the finest products of the Cretan workshops were the jars and vases in which the Minoans stored olive oil and wine. The introduction of the potter's wheel to the island early in the second millennium had fostered a remarkable development in

the art of pottery. Craftsmen learned to make the famous 'egg-shell ware', beautifully decorated vessels of exceptional delicacy, with walls that were literally almost as thin as eggshells. The painting of vases became a fine art, and a variety of forms was evolved, many of them highly sophisticated. In the later periods, vases became more ornate; they were adorned with fanciful blossoms made of clay and baked on to the outer surface. The Minoan pottery that survives today remains one of the finest manifestations of the island's culture. Indeed, it deserves to rank among the most beautiful that has ever been made.

The Minoans would not have been able to develop such a rich and powerful civilization but for their extensive maritime trade. Their neolithic ancestors had arrived by sea, and they themselves became a great seafaring people. 'The first person known to us by tradition as having established a navy is Minos,' wrote that most reliable historian, Thucydides.

> He made himself master of what is now called the Hellenic sea, and ruled over the Cyclades [islands between Greece and Asia Minor], into most of which he sent the first colonies ... appointing his own sons as governors; and thus did his best to put down piracy in those waters, a necessary step to secure the revenues for his own use.

There is abundant evidence of Minoan ports and other coastal settlements, for example at Amnisos, which appears to have been a port for Knossos, and at Nirou Khani, another port four miles farther to the east. There is also another harbour at the mouth of the river Kairatos, two miles west of Amnisos. Three harbours within a short distance of the northern capital suggest a large fleet and much sea-borne trade. Even in early Minoan times representations of ships appear frequently on bead seals; the remains of wharves at Nirou Khani are in fact the most ancient harbour works ever discovered along the shores of the Mediterranean.

The excavations at Crete have revealed no signs of fortifications, which suggests that Minoan maritime power freed the island from the fear of foreign invasion. That the Minoans colonized the Cyclades, as Thucydides believed, seems

A terracotta provision jar still stands among the ruins of the palace of Mallia.

Golden pendant representing two hornets with wings raised.

unlikely, although they may have exercised some control over local settlements there. One must be careful in claiming that the Minoans controlled the seas by means of a formidable navy. The Minos of whom Thucydides wrote could have been an Achaean from the mainland, for at a somewhat later period a confederacy controlled from the mainland did in fact dominate the eastern Mediterranean. Nevertheless there is ample evidence that long before the mainland Achaeans occupied Crete, the Minoans traded extensively in the eastern Mediterranean, with the Aegean Islands, the Greek mainland, Malta, Cyprus, Syria, and Palestine, as well as with Egypt. There is evidence of Minoan activity to the west as far as Sicily. To what extent the early Cretans established colonies is uncertain, but many of their trading posts in various distant places did become permanent settlements. Thucydides was apparently not far wrong, though he wrote more than a thousand years after the events he described.

The material remains of Minoan civilization are like a palimpsest, in which one picture has been painted over another, and another one above that. The picture provided by the remains of palaces at Knossos, Phaistos, and Mallia is the uppermost one, representing the ultimate phase of that civilization just before it was destroyed about 1400 B.C. (though minority opinion favours a later date). After revealing these heights of accomplishment Evans and other archaeologists set about the more difficult task of uncovering the beginnings of this earliest civilization in Europe, and of tracing it through successive stages from neolithic times down to the Late Bronze Age. In this Evans was the most fortunate, since the lowest levels of the mound on which Knossos stands go back to before 3000 B.C. The examination of these levels was aided by the fact that some of them contained Egyptian objects which could be dated with relative precision. Evans eventually worked out a chronological system for Minoan history which he divided into early, middle, and late periods, extending roughly from the beginning of the Old Kingdom in Egypt through the Middle and New Kingdoms (about 2700–1100 B.C.). Each of these broad divisions was subdivided into three sections, based mainly on changes in pottery styles. This system, first presented in 1904, is still generally accepted, although in recent years disputes have arisen over the dating of various periods and particularly over the dating of the last years that witnessed the decline of Minoan civilization.

There are hundreds of islands in the east Mediterranean, three of them – Rhodes, Crete, and Cyprus – of considerable size. A large number of these islands has been occupied by human beings at least since the Early Bronze Age. Crete was the only one to achieve an indigenous civilization as highly developed as the other great contemporary civilizations we have been considering – those of Egypt, Mesopotamia, and the Indus Valley. These three grew up along fertile river valleys. But Crete is a mountainous island with no large rivers and few plants of any size. What, then, were the conditions that favoured the development of such a highly distinctive culture and that allowed it to flourish for so long a time?

There is no certain answer, but we can distinguish a number of factors that probably contributed. The most important of these is Crete's geographic position. Both Rhodes and Cyprus are near Anatolia, and Cyprus is not far from Syria; both were subject to invasion and strong foreign influence from early times, whereas Crete – 'out in the wine-dark sea', as Homer says – was sufficiently remote from the nearest civilized power, Egypt, to develop an independent culture. Yet it was near enough to Africa and Asia to receive influences from both continents via trade and the peaceful immigration of people, some of whom brought with them new techniques, notably bronzeworking.

Another interesting fact, pointed out by Spyridon Marinatos, is that even in remote antiquity Crete had few dangerous or noxious animals. The ancient Greeks said that Heracles had cleansed Crete of 'wild animals like bears, wolves, snakes, and the like'. This is not true of snakes; there are some, including a poisonous variety, and scorpions are common. But whereas the Greek mainland and some of the Aegean Islands had wolves, foxes, bears, lions, and boars, Crete's wild animals most likely consisted only of the harmless mountain goat and the porcupine. To primitive settlers this relative absence of dangerous and destructive animals would have been an advantage. Again, Crete has sufficient cultivable land to support a considerable population. The soil of the plains is fertile, and in many places the lower slopes of the hills can be terraced and cultivated.

In ancient times, forests of oak, fir, cypress, and cedar, which have long since disappeared, provided an abundance of timber for fuel and for building. They also helped to conserve the winter rainfall which nowadays rushes down the mountain slopes, scouring off the topsoil and exposing the arid, ochre-coloured rocks so characteristic of the present Cretan landscape. The abundant springs that once nourished the soil have largely dried up. Crete is still a 'rich and lovely land', as Homer describes it, but in 3000 B.C. it must have been much more fertile than it is today.

We do not know precisely when Crete was first settled. It is conceivable, however, that between 5000 and 4000 B.C. people who possessed stone tools and who practised agriculture and stock-raising had begun to move into Greece and some of the Aegean Islands. It does seem almost certain that most of the early immigrants came from the east, where these skills

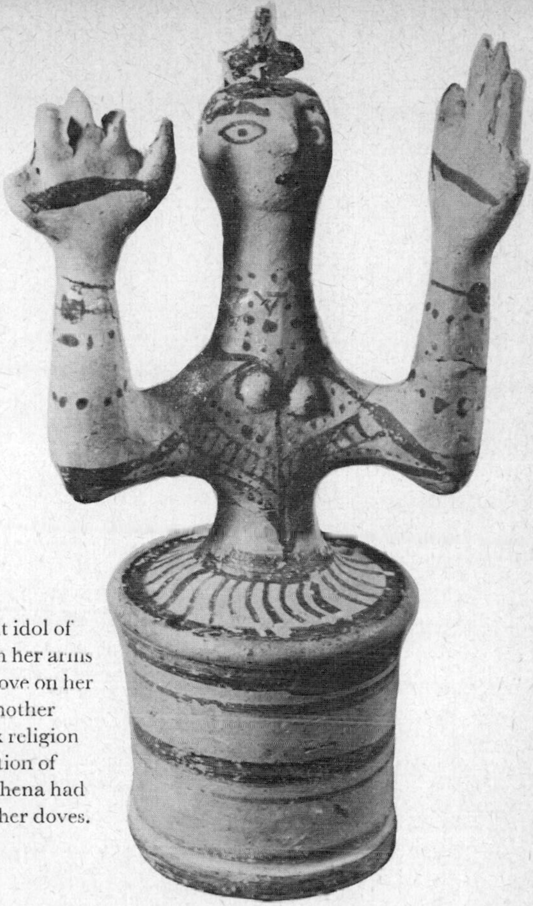

This image may be a cult idol of the mother goddess, with her arms raised in blessing. The dove on her head was sacred to the mother goddess, and later Greek religion continued the identification of goddesses with birds; Athena had her owl, and Aphrodite her doves.

and techniques were understood. Some would have come from Asia Minor; others may have sailed from Syria and Palestine, or even from Egypt and Libya. Judging from their pottery styles they did not all come from the same place or at the same time; one must imagine a slow infiltration by relatively small groups. By 3000 B.C. some of these wandering peoples had settled in Crete. Their remains have been found in caves, which were their homes and which also sometimes served as burial places. In some respects their pottery is not unlike pottery of the same period found in Palestine. They fashioned crude clay figurines, possibly of a mother goddess. But not much more is known of these neolithic inhabitants of the island.

During the five centuries following 3000 B.C. the Cretan settlers prospered, multiplied, and gradually spread over most of the island, though they remained largely concentrated on the Messara plain and in eastern Crete. Even at this early stage they were in touch with Egypt (indeed, as earlier suggested, some settlers may have come from there) and Egyptian stone vases of the Predynastic and Early Dynastic Periods have been found on the island. The Cretans learned to make excellent stone vessels for themselves, judging from some handsome examples that have been discovered in veined limestone, in polychrome steatite, and in other stones. They made palettes for grinding eye paint, an idea which may also have come from predynastic Egypt. They grew the papyrus plant, and sugar cane, which a tradition claims was brought to Crete by the ancient Egyptians.

These people learned to build settlements with houses of complex plan and with many rooms. They raised herds of oxen, sheep, and swine, kept fowl, grew corn and vines, and cultivated the olive tree. They seem never to have suffered foreign invasion, although they were beset by earthquakes and had to learn to strengthen their buildings by a half-timber construction. A bountiful supply of wood made this method the easiest for the Cretans to use.

The earliest copper implements found in the Minoan graves were imported. But by about 2500 B.C. there appear moulds for making tools and weapons of this metal, proving that the craft of metalworking had reached the island, as indeed it had the Greek mainland. It was the dawn of the Aegean Bronze Age.

Some archaeologists have suggested that the change from stone to metal tools may have been precipitated by political disturbances in Egypt. At the end of the Sixth Dynasty, about 2200 B.C., the Old Kingdom was destroyed, and as we have seen, there was both civil strife and an invasion of foreigners in the Delta. Sinclair Hood suggests that at this time there was a mass migration of peoples from Anatolia down the coast of Syria and Palestine towards Egypt, and that in the resultant disturbances refugees may have crossed over to Crete and other Aegean islands. Although Crete had been trading with Egypt

Known as the Chieftain's Cup, this steatite vase shows a helmeted officer standing before a man who may be a prince.

from a very early date, contacts became closer and more frequent, and reciprocal influences become increasingly evident in the arts and crafts of both countries.

Some Cretan ships with high prows seem to have closely resembled Egyptian vessels. By the beginning of the Egyptian Twelfth Dynasty, about 2000 B.C., the Cretans were imitating Egyptian scarabs and other objects, and slightly later Minoan pottery, with Minoan fashions in decoration, was being exported to Egypt. But there were other influences affecting Crete, represented, for instance, by a characteristically Anatolian jug with a spout, which appeared first in Greece and then in Crete. It is reasonable to assume that Minoan civilization throughout its development gathered ideas and techniques from both African and Asian sources, but adapted them to its own use.

But one fact must be made clear. Though we speak of the 'Greek' mainland, up until about 1900 B.C. (the date must remain very approximate) both Greece and the Aegean Islands were occupied by people who spoke non-Greek languages. Names ending in *-ssos*, such as Knossos and Tylissos, or those ending in *-inth*, such as Corinth and labyrinth, belong to a group of non-Greek languages. Similar word endings appear in

Anatolia, especially in the names of mountains and rivers. This strongly suggests that the pre-Greek inhabitants of the Aegean Islands and the mainland spoke the same language (or group of languages) as the peoples of Anatolia, whence some of their ancestors may have come.

Was there a written form for the Cretan language, as there was for the Egyptian and Sumerian languages of the period? A primitive form of writing, in the shape of simple pictographs, has been detected on seal stones and clay tablets of the Early Bronze Age in Crete, though there is as yet little evidence that it existed on the mainland. But there is no doubt that it was this script that later developed into what Evans called Linear A, one of the two linear systems that he recognized on the Knossian tablets. It was a syllabary, in which each sign represented the syllable of a word. Linear A has been found only in Crete; the various attempts at translation that have thus far been made, as well as conjectures regarding its ultimate origins, remain a matter of debate.

The introduction of bronzeworking into Crete had revolutionary effects; the advantage of metal weapons and implements is obvious. Crete developed its own characteristic variety of spears and daggers, and metal tools gave new powers to the stonemason and the carpenter. Instead of rough stone, builders were able to use finely cut ashlar masonry, which they did mainly for the outer walls of palaces and great houses; copper and bronze saws made it easier to fell trees and cut up the timber into suitable lengths for the framework of buildings. However, the metal was expensive; metal vessels were imitated in pottery and stone tools continued to be used for a long period.

By 2000 B.C. the island civilization was well established, and most of its characteristic features had appeared. It was at this stage that the foundations of the first palaces at Knossos, Phaistos, and Mallia were laid. Hitherto there had been extensive settlements at each of these places, but nothing resembling the residence of a king. Then, apparently quite suddenly, the Cretans began building enormous residential and administrative units for their rulers. Several hundred years later the palaces were destroyed and new structures

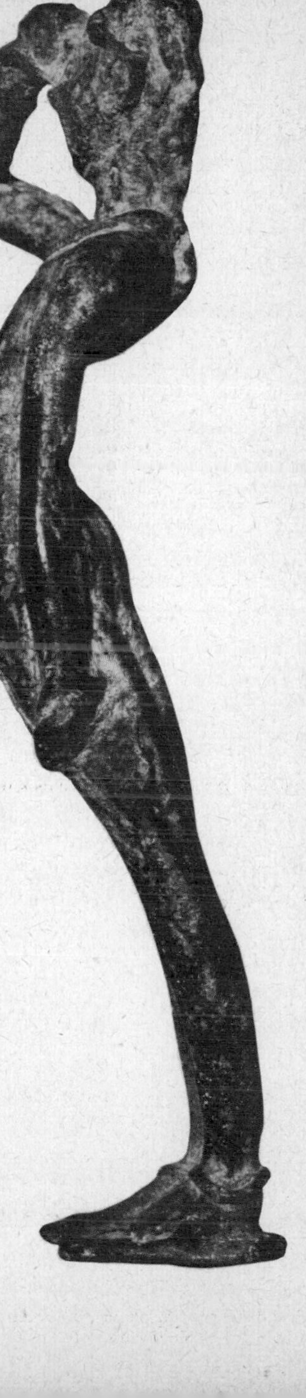

Votive offering, representing a
worshipper, his hand reverently raised.

Probably participating in a religious ceremony, three women dance in a ring around a lyre player. They form part of a votive group that once may have represented a complete circle of dancers.

were raised on the same sites, but enough of the earlier buildings was incorporated into the later ones to provide the excavators with some indication of their character. The early palaces at Knossos, Phaistos, and Mallia had three courts, a large rectangular one around which were grouped the main buildings, a second to the west, and a third, smaller court to the north. The main court was oriented on a north–south axis, and the general layout of the buildings was similar to that of the palaces that were later built on the site.

No one has yet satisfactorily explained the sudden innovation of those first palaces. There is no evidence of an invasion by newcomers who could have brought with them a tradition of monumental architecture; it might be that by this time, at the opening of the second millennium, power had become sufficiently centralized to make it possible for three potent chiefs each to set up an administrative unit, controlling an area from which it drew its wealth. Who these rulers were we do not know, though one is reminded of the Greek legend that stated that Zeus had three sons by Europa – Minos, Sarpedon, and Rhadamanthus.

No doubt these palaces, like those of later periods that replaced them, had shrines that served for formal worship of the established royal cult. Elsewhere on the island – on mountaintops, in sacred groves with walled enclosures, in caves, and most frequently in rock shelters – archaeologists have discovered sanctuaries that were evidently cult centres of the popular religion.

From the innumerable votive offerings left in such sanctuaries by worshippers almost four thousand years ago, we can speculate on the nature of Minoan religion. There are little clay figures representing the familiar Minoan man tightly belted and wearing a loincloth, and with a typical Cretan dagger at his waist (the men of Crete still wear daggers). There are delightful figurines of women wearing long, full skirts, like the representations of goddesses we have considered earlier – and, also like the goddesses, naked from the waist up. The hair dos of these ladies, it might be noted, are varied and enchanting.

Some votive offerings clearly reveal the occupation of the donor. One clay bowl represents a shepherd with his flock; another with a flying bird may be the offering of a wild-fowler asking the goddess to grant him success in his hunting. There are many painted cattle, and most significant of all, statuettes of bulls with little human figures clinging to their horns. One has a young man, apparently naked, hanging on to one of the bull's horns as he strives to maintain a grip on its neck with his legs. On a later seal stone a bull is shown kneeling (perhaps it is tethered) while an acrobat grabs the horns and leaps over its back. Could this have been an athlete in training? The more one studies these fascinating little figures the more one wonders whether the palace performances, as depicted in the Knossos fresco, which must have involved elaborate training and a formal ritual, originated as a sport among the young herdsmen of the plains.

The deity to whom these offerings are made is a goddess, probably the same goddess under different aspects – as queen of the animals, the sea, the mountains, or the infernal powers. Sometimes she is shown with a bird, at other times with a flower, the horns of consecration, or a snake – as in the faience figure from the Knossos shrine. To caves high up in the mountains, so high that in winter they are snow-bound, the Cretans made their toilsome way with their offerings. In those gloomy

One of a group of models representing the bull games, the ivory acrobat at top was shown leaping over a bull. The bull leaper's most difficult feat, shown in the bronze below, required him to grasp the bull's horns and somersault over its back.

caverns, where the glistening stalactites and stalagmites reflected the flickering lamps of the worshippers and bats fluttered in the shadows, they must have felt very close to their deity. Even today these caves are hardly less mysterious, since few visitors have the stamina needed to reach them, and one treads about on piles of fragmented pottery left there over three thousand years ago. Some caves have enclosing walls and the remains of altars, and from time to time new caves are discovered which sometimes yield hoards of bronze objects and pottery. No doubt still more await discovery. Everywhere in Crete, in palaces and in remote caves, one encounters evidence of religious worship or observances; but the evidence is never monumental. Unlike their contemporaries in Egypt and Mesopotamia, the Cretans built no great temples and they raised no large statues of their deities. Unlike the Egyptians and the Mesopotamians, we might conclude, the Minoans were not unduly awed by the supernatural.

Minoan civilization appears to have enjoyed its greatest flowering between about 1700 and 1400 B.C. Early in this period the great palaces were rebuilt and the first large mansions were raised. It was the remains of these later palaces that first claimed the attention of Evans, Halbherr, and other excavators. Why there was need for rebuilding has not been satisfactorily explained. However, Crete has been subject to earthquakes at fairly regular intervals during the past seven hundred years at least, and presumably this was so in ancient

Although little is known about the cult of the dead in Crete, a painting on a sarcophagus discovered at Hagia Triada has been interpreted as representing the veneration of a dead man, whose effigy or body appears at far right. As a musician plays upon his lyre, two women offer libations. Beside them three men bring other offerings to the deceased man – two calves and, following contemporary Egyptian practice, a funeral boat as well. At far left can be seen two high pillars supporting double axes; the birds that are shown perched on them could be representations of the mother goddess, but are more probably spirits of the dead.

times as well. Such tremors may well have damaged the earlier structures. Evans, who found evidences of frequent rebuilding at Knossos, became absorbed by this problem, particularly when he came upon a part of the Knossian palace that bore clear evidence of earthquake damage and that had been rebuilt after due sacrifice to the infernal powers. He carefully examined the records of earthquakes that had occurred during the past seven centuries.

> That space of time [he wrote] almost exactly corresponds with the duration of the great Minoan palace in its successive phases, and we are almost bound to infer that the same natural forces must largely account for the signs of ruin that here mark the successive stages of the building.

One day in April 1922, when Evans's workmen had just cleared the remains of the so-called House of the Sacrifice in which bulls had evidently been sacrificed to the earth goddess, there came suddenly

> a short, sharp shock, sufficient to throw one of my men backwards, [which was] accompanied by a deep, rumbling sound . . . experienced on the site and throughout the entire region.

In Minoan Crete the trident, emblem of the god Poseidon, the 'earth-shaker', often appears. Evans recalled that Homer had written in the twentieth book of the *Iliad*, 'in bulls does the earth-shaker delight'. In 1900, just as Evans had arrived to begin digging at Knossos, he had been welcomed by Zeus with one of the fiercest thunderstorms within living memory. Twenty-six years later, in 1926, Poseidon the 'earth-shaker' was also to manifest his menacing power. On a warm summer night in June Sir Arthur was resting in one of the basement rooms of his house, the Villa Ariadne. He wrote,

> My own mind was thus full of past earthquakes and the foreboding of a new convulsion when on June 26 last, at 9.45 in the evening of a calm, warm day, the shocks began. They caught me reading on my bed in a basement room ... and, trusting to the exceptional strength of the fabric, I chose to see the earthquake through from within. ...

The movement, which recalled a ship in a storm, though only of a minute and a quarter's duration, already began to produce the same physical effect on me as a rough sea. A dull sound rose from the ground like the muffled roar of an angry bull; our single bell rang, while through the open window came the more distant jangling of the chimes of Candia Cathedral. . . .

It is something to have heard with one's own ears the bellowing of the bull beneath the earth who, according to a primitive belief, tosses it with its horns. It was doubtless the constant need of protection against these petulant bursts of the infernal powers that explains the Minoan tendency to concentrate their worship on the chthonic aspect of their great goddess, wreathed with serpents as Lady of the Underworld.

Evans, despite his great gifts and dedicated labours over thirty years, may have been wrong in some of his conclusions concerning Minoan Crete. But his burning imagination and insight break through in those words.

The last, most catastrophic destruction of the Minoan structures is generally believed to have taken place about 1450 B.C. when virtually every centre was ruined, except Knossos which survived another half century. Then it too was destroyed. At Knossos and a number of other sites on the island there are the unmistakable marks of fire. Evans believed that after this disaster Minoan civilization went into a rapid decline, although some sort of life continued at Knossos during what he called the Reoccupation Period, from 1400 to 1100 B.C., when 'squatters' occupied the great palace. But Phaistos, Mallia, and other centres did not revive.

The main question, of course, is what caused this final destruction? Was it, as Evans suggested, an earthquake, such as Crete had suffered before? Or was it, as others have believed, the result of armed attack? There are various reasons for believing that the island suffered a sacking by hostile invaders. Minoan civilization had, after all, recovered from earlier disasters caused by earthquakes, but this time it did not survive the calamity. Also, in modern cities, with their gas and electricity supplies, earthquakes often cause catastrophic fires, but this was not necessarily true in the ancient world. Yet many Minoan settlements apparently went up in flames at about the same time; charred timber and smoke-blackened oil jars show this only too clearly, suggesting that the palaces may have been deliberately set on fire after sacking. At this time, it is certain, the Mycenaeans of the mainland were powerful and warlike. After the destruction of Knossos they became dominant in the Aegean, and Minoan influence practically disappeared.

The late J. D. S. Pendlebury, who for years was Evans's assistant at Knossos, favoured the 'sack' theory, and thought he saw evidence of it in the condition of the Throne Room, where ritual vases had been overturned, as if, in his own words,

> [they] were in the act of being used when the disaster came. It looks as if the king had been hurried there to undergo too late some last ceremony in the hope of saving the people. Theseus and the Minotaur! Dare we believe that he wore the mask of a bull?

That the Theseus of legend represents the leader of an armed invasion by Mycenaeans, and that he overcame King Minos, wearing the mask of a bull as he performed some hasty last rite, is a romantic conjecture. As Pendlebury conceded, 'Such imaginings may not be suitable to archaeology.' But, he added, 'with this possibility in mind, I defy anyone to enter the Throne Room without a strange thrill'.

As discussed at greater length in the following chapter, the question is made more complicated by the fact that many tablets found amid the ruins of Knossos were inscribed in the Linear B script. According to the recent decipherment of the script, Linear B records an early form of the Greek language used by the Mycenaeans. This at least indicates the possibility of strong Mycenaean influence at Knossos some time before the destruction of the palace. Other theories suggest that there was a civil uprising within Crete, perhaps assisted by foreign invaders, or simply another earthquake that struck Crete at a time when her civilization was already in decline, and from which the Cretans were unable to recover. Marinatos combines two of these theories by suggesting that the Mycenaeans exploited the confusion caused by the earthquake to occupy the island, and then set up an Achaean prince to rule at Knossos.

When Homer composed the *Odyssey* in the eighth century B.C., Crete was a relatively unimportant island in the Mediterranean world, but legends of its past had persisted over the centuries. In the cosmopolitan and densely populated world of Crete, 'out in the wine-dark sea', as Homer describes it,

Each of the several races of the isle has its own language. First there are the Achaeans; then the genuine Cretans, proud of their native stock; next the Cydonians; the Dorians, with their three clans; and finally the noble Pelasgians.

Homer purported to describe the Crete of the years after the Trojan War, when, we assume, the Achaeans still ruled the Aegean. But to round off his story he obviously drew on materials that had survived from various stages of the island's history, as well as on the reports of his contemporaries, who may have seen the island. Among his sources may have been fragments of stories that reached far back to the time when Minoan culture was at the height of its glory. It is tempting to surmise that his description of the island of Phaeacia, on which Odysseus is shipwrecked and where he meets the fair Nausicaä, may hold memories of the fascinating Minoan world that Evans rediscovered at Knossos just two short generations ago.

The king of the island explains to his stranded guest that his people

can run fast and . . . are first-rate seamen. But the things in which we take a perennial delight are the feast, the lyre, the dance, clean linen in plenty, a hot bath, and our beds.

In another passage Nausicaä, the king's daughter, says,

there is no man on earth, nor ever will be, who would dare to set hostile feet on Phaeacian soil. The gods are too fond of us for that. Remote in this sea-beaten home of ours, we are the outposts of mankind. . . .

Phaeacia may have been an imaginary island, but the emphasis on remoteness – 'the outposts of mankind' – maritime skill – 'first-rate seamen' – and the uninhibited delight in the luxuries of civilization – 'the feast, the lyre, the dance, clean linen in plenty, a hot bath, and our beds' – are all suggestive enough of the evidence revealed by Evans from his excavations in Crete.

The Minoans, like the Etruscans, suffer from having their history written by others. Unlike the later Greeks, or the Egyptians, the Sumerians, the Babylonians, or the Assyrians, they cannot speak to us directly – at least not until their Linear A script is thoroughly translated, and possibly not even then. We are left only with buildings, frescoes, bead seals, pottery, and the superb Cretan landscape, which is still wide enough, high enough, and remote enough to excite our imagination.

2 Mycenae The World of Heroes

According to Greek mythology Thessaly, in the northern part of modern Greece, was the birthplace of gods; it was the legendary scene of the creation and of the flood, and the home of the wise Centaurs. It was also the home of the great immortals who dwelt on Mount Olympus, the highest of the mountains that hem in the broad, fertile Thessalian plains. We do not know when the first mortals settled in Greece but, significantly, the earliest remains of human activity in that land, which date from palaeolithic times, have been found in Thessaly and in near-by Boeotia.

In Thessaly there were also numerous neolithic settlements. One such, at Dimini near modern Volos, consisted of a number of relatively simple dwellings grouped around the house of the local ruler. The inhabitants grew barley, wheat, some fruits and vegetables, and raised cattle, pigs, sheep, and goats. Even at this early date they apparently found it necessary to fortify their settlement with concentric walls, evidence of the insecurity so long felt by the mainland people but virtually unknown among the early Minoans of sea-girt Crete.

The chief's house at Dimini was of a type that occurs in

The Lion Gate.

more developed form again and again on the Greek mainland. An open court led to a porch, beyond which lay the main two-room building. This would appear to be the ancestor of characteristic structures found by excavators at later palace sites, incorporating the kind of kingly hall that was uncovered at Mycenae, Pylos, and Tiryns. This type of building occurs somewhat later at Troy, and elsewhere in Anatolia. From this it is assumed that the early settlers in Greece had strong ties with that land; some of them may have come from there. (Troy stood at a strategic point commanding the passage of the Dardanelles, which lay athwart the important land route from the western Anatolian coast to Greece.)

There are no written records, but it is confidently assumed that these settlers of some five thousand years ago were not Greeks, that is they did not speak the Greek language. Schliemann's excavations at Mycenae and subsequent investigations there and at different sites on the mainland, on the other hand, revealed a vigorous and in many ways distinctive Late Bronze Age culture of Greek-speaking peoples. Judging from the findings in the shaft graves this so-called Mycenaean civilization burgeoned suddenly and dramatically about the turn of the sixteenth century B.C. and flourished for four centuries or more. Particularly in its early stages it showed strong influences from Minoan Crete. Later, from about 1400 to 1200 B.C., it became itself a dominant influence in the Aegean area and beyond. Then, shortly after the Trojan War, it rapidly declined, leaving only legends of its glory and the ruins of its impressive monuments.

The main questions to be answered are: when did the first Greek-speaking people enter Greece; where did they come from; what was their level of culture; what were their relations with the Minoans of Crete; and what accounts for the sudden deterioration of their civilization? These questions can be only partly answered. At the beginning of the second millennium B.C. high civilization was just beginning, both in Crete and on the mainland. Bronze was coming into use, of course. Outside Athens, at the site of an early fortified town that dates as far back as the third millennium, moulds for casting bronze implements, weapons, and other objects and the remains of smelting furnaces have been found. Other of the sites later called Mycenaean, such as Mycenae itself, the stronghold of Agamemnon, had been occupied longer. But little has been learned of the pre-Greek inhabitants of this city; because it was built on rock and was frequently enlarged, its stratification is archaeologically frustrating and earlier levels are difficult to establish. Nevertheless, according to the late archaeologist Alan Wace, who dug for many years at Mycenae, the plentiful pottery finds there prove that the site was occupied by 3000 B.C. Tiryns and Pylos were also old, established communities. There are remains of an immense circular building at Tiryns that date back five thousand years, but they underlie a later Mycenaean palace and have not been explored. Many of these sites are in the Peloponnesus, in southern Greece, where prehistoric settlements were often built on rocky eminences.

Between 2000 and 1700 B.C., when the first palaces were being built in Crete, the mainland was subject to waves of invasion or immigration. Most specialists in Aegean archaeology believe that the newcomers were the first Greek-speaking people to enter Greece. These people could have come there from somewhere in the north. From Schliemann's time, the legend of blonde Aryans from northern Europe who invaded Greece and founded a warrior aristocracy such as that described by Homer has had many adherents. It flatters Anglo-Saxon vanity that Homer refers to 'the fair-haired Achaeans', and that 'the fair Helen' might have been a Nordic blonde.

But there is little evidence to support the theory that these first Greeks were of such origins. It seems more probable that, like the earlier settlers, they came from Anatolia. In passing, it is worth mention that the invaders of Greece brought with them a pottery-making technique, represented by a drab but highly distinctive product known as Grey Minyan Ware, that they shared with but one other people – the people who invaded Troy and settled there at this same time, roughly about 1950 B.C. This ware was also known to the neighbouring areas of western Anatolia that fell within the range of Trojan influence.

Wherever they came from, whatever dialect they spoke, the immigrants early in the second millennium came within the cultural sphere of the Minoans of Crete. Until the evidence

The Minoan fertility goddess appears on the face of this Mycenaean gold signet ring. There is a bird behind her chair; before her are stalks of wheat and a procession of demons bearing water.

has been studied further and the results made known, it is difficult to judge the exact relationship of the two cultures over the next several hundred years. However, during the sixteenth and fifteenth centuries B.C., when Minoan culture was at the height of its development, its artistic influence on the mainland became widespread.

Sir Arthur Evans believed and maintained to the end of his life that the Cretans colonized not only the islands of the Aegean, but also parts of the Greek mainland, and that such centres as Mycenae and Tiryns were originally Minoan dependencies. It seems a sound enough theory; many of the objects found in the Mycenaean shaft graves, which can be dated between 1600 and 1500 B.C., are surely from Crete or at least were made by Cretan craftsmen. Others imitate the styles of Crete. There are gold signet rings with typically Minoan scenes of goddesses; the warriors or huntsmen represented on gold-inlaid daggers are tightly belted in the Minoan manner and carry Minoan figure-of-eight shields; and there is a bull's-head rhyton that is highly reminiscent of such a vessel unearthed at Knossos. All this glory suddenly begins to appear in these burials of the sixteenth century B.C.; the earlier graves

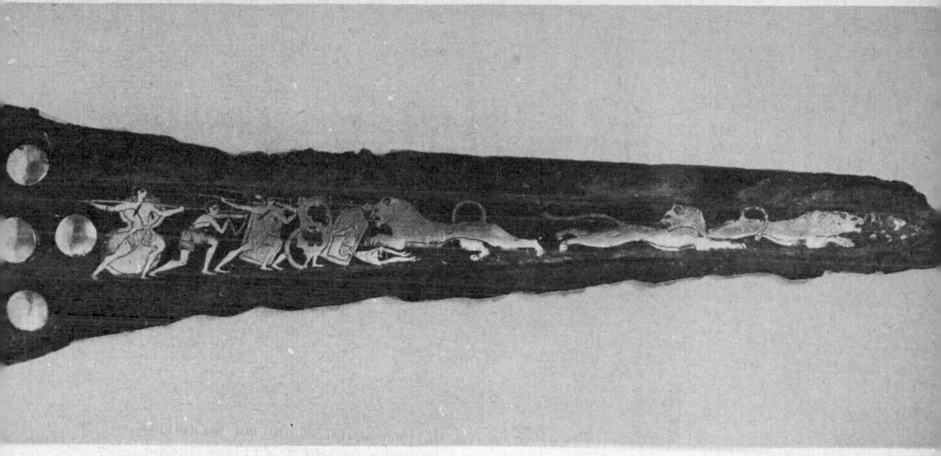

Although lions never existed in Crete, they did live on the Greek mainland; representations of them were common in Aegean art, and stories about them occur in Greek mythology. The Mycenaeans were profoundly impressed by the power of the beast: its image may have been placed over the main gateway at Mycenae as a symbol of divine protection. This bronze dagger shows a group of huntsmen attacking a formidable lion, who is about to maul one of his attackers. The hunters are armed as if for warfare; two of them carry figure-of-eight shields, which the Mycenaeans may have adopted from Crete. The two other shields shown are of the rectangular type that was most commonly used by the Homeric warriors; like the figure-of-eight shields, they were suspended over the shoulders with a strap so that both arms could be left free for fighting. Inlaid with silver and gold, the dagger is a ceremonial weapon, probably of Cretan workmanship. The hunters shown on it have their waists tightly bound and wear costumes similar to those that were worn in Crete.

discovered at Mycenae are pitifully small, furnished at most with a few funeral offerings.

Yet there was opposition to Evans's point of view, led chiefly by Wace, who worked for many years at Mycenae. He and others pointed out that there were substantial differences between Mycenaean and Cretan palaces, bespeaking distinctive cultural heritages. At Mycenae, Tiryns, and the later-discovered Pylos, the principal architectural feature was not the central court of the Cretan palaces, but the megaron – a squarish hall that contained the king's throne and a large, fixed circular hearth in the centre. This hearth was surrounded by four pillars which supported the roof; sometimes there was a second, smaller megaron, possibly for the queen, and a staircase leading to an upper storey.

The best-preserved example of such a megaron is at Pylos in the Palace of Nestor, most venerable of the Homeric leaders in the *Iliad*. It is very like the building described by Nausicaä when she directs Odysseus to her father's palace.

> Directly you have passed through the courtyard and into the buildings, walk quickly through the great hall [megaron] until you reach my mother, who generally sits in the firelight by the hearth, weaving yarn stained with sea-purple, and forming a delightful picture, with her chair against a pillar and her maids sitting behind. My father's throne is close to hers, and there he sits drinking his wine like a god.

As in the early building at Dimini and its Anatolian analogues, the principal megaron was usually approached via an open courtyard and a pillared porch. In another passage Homer tells of Telemachus who, searching for news of his father, visits Menelaus in Sparta and spends the night there 'in the portico' of the palace – on the porch, we may assume – while Menelaus sleeps in his room 'beside the lovely Helen'. Homer also describes the hearth at which Menelaus sits and where he is joined by Helen, no longer the *femme fatale*, but a model of domestic propriety – though it may be noted in passing that she still needs three handmaidens to carry the sewing, and that her workbasket runs 'on casters and [is] made of silver finished with a rim of gold'.

At this time, buildings of the Mycenaean plan did not exist in Crete. There the palaces consisted of many rooms opening off a central courtyard. There was no permanent central hearth and no principal porch like those of mainland structures. The influences that shaped Mycenaean civilization came from various sources besides the neighbouring island of Crete. The two famous grave circles with their royal shaft graves, discovered by Schliemann and John Papadimitriou at Mycenae, have predecessors seven hundred years older at Alaja Huyuk in central Anatolia. Further, as Sinclair Hood comments, 'the shaft graves show a striking mixture of the barbaric and the civilized'. Aside from the artifacts that reflect the sophisticated taste of contemporary Crete, there are, for instance, amber beads that may have come from the Baltic. Some of the metalwork seems to stem from the Caucasus or the northern steppes rather than from the Aegean. The horse-drawn chariots that appear on the Mycenaean grave stelae were certainly not representations of anything Cretan; they came from western Asia.

However, the influence of Minoan art was pervasive and enduring. What accounts for this? Cretan gold- and bronzework could have been acquired either by peaceful trading contacts or by looting Minoan settlements, by inducing Cretan craftsmen to work on the mainland or by carrying them off as slaves and obliging them to do so. Examples are not lacking from later times of hardy, less developed people acquiring a taste for more civilized living, and so it may have been in prehistoric Greece. As one scholar has pointed out, the influence of Minoan art on the Mycenaeans, so dramatically demonstrated by the finds in the shaft graves, may represent nothing more than a newly adopted fashion. It does not necessarily mean that Crete dominated and controlled the mainland. In eighteenth-century Europe there was a great craze for chinoiserie, but this does not indicate a Chinese conquest of Europe. It should be noted, however, that Minoan art continued to be in fashion on the mainland over the course of many centuries.

Then there is the knotty question of Homeric parallels, first raised by Schliemann. The traditional date of the Trojan War is the beginning of the twelfth century B.C., although recent studies place it a half century or more earlier. The *Odyssey* and the *Iliad* were probably composed about four hundred years later. Both poems are a strange mixture, portraying partly the society that Homer himself knew, and partly an archaic way of life that resembles the one revealed by the excavations at Mycenae and similar sites. We read of bronze swords, of chariots, and of Hector's great ox-hide shield, which tapped his neck and his ankles as he walked. On the inlaid daggers found in the shaft graves at Mycenae are depicted large body shields just like those described in the *Iliad*. The buildings and ivory-mounted furniture that have been unearthed are remarkably like those lovingly described by Homer.

Although much Mycenaean pottery imitated Cretan styles, the use of scenes from daily life for the decoration of vases was a Mycenaean innovation; this fragment shows two warriors driving a chariot.

His description of a golden cup decorated with feeding doves is, again, very like an actual example found in a shaft grave; and his account of a formidable helmet strengthened by slivers of boars' tusks closely corresponds to those represented on several Mycenaean ivories.

Yet in Homer's own time warriors no longer fought from chariots, they used iron rather than bronze weapons, and they carried much smaller shields. And certainly during the so-called Dark Age when these two epics took final shape, kings and rulers did not possess either palaces or furnishings of the richness attributed by Homer to the kings of Mycenae, Pylos, Sparta, and Troy at the time of the Trojan War.

A Mycenaean warrior, carved of ivory, wears a boar's-tusk helmet and carries a figure-of-eight shield.

A fresco discovered at Tiryns shows greyhounds attacking a boar that has been wounded by a hunter's spear. Rows of boars' teeth were often used as armour on helmets; going into battle against the Trojans, Odysseus wore a helmet covered with them.

Homer drew on legends that had been transmitted orally from generation to generation for centuries past. Among these were stories of gods and heroes, and of people who may actually have lived – men who fought in the Trojan War, and kings and princes who had dwelt in the palaces of Mycenaean cities that in Homer's own day were for the most part little more than ruins. He composed these tales into two great epics, the *Iliad* and *Odyssey*. The first tells of the 'wrath of Achilles' and describes the Trojan War; the second deals with the wanderings of Odysseus and his return to his home in Ithaca. But it is very apparent that Homer was only using part of the material available to him. Other, later poets, such as Hesiod, and Greek dramatists of the classical periods, such as Aeschylus, Sophocles, and Euripides, had access to the same material and tell us stories that Homer does not mention. All must be based to some extent on the Mycenaean civilization that has been revealed by archaeologists. When Homer described the hall in which Odysseus slew the suitors of Penelope, he was no doubt using the description of an earlier poet who had seen and perhaps actually sung in such halls.

But he drew also from the life he saw about him, from his observed experience. So in one part of the *Iliad* he has Agamemnon carrying spears characteristic of Homer's own day. The four-horse chariot described in the story of Nestor's war in Elis seems to have been an innovation of the eighth century B.C. Throughout, the Homeric stories are laid over with such 'modern' embroidery, details that were present knowledge only to those who lived four or five centuries after the hey-day of Mycenaean heroes.

The Homeric epics and some of the later writings on the same theme deal not only with the Trojan War but with the events that preceded and followed it. For instance, Aeschylus, in his trilogy the *Oresteia*, tells how Agamemnon, king of Mycenae and leader of the Greek host, who had sacrificed his daughter Iphigenia to obtain fair winds for his expedition to Troy, was slain upon his return by his wife, Clytemnestra, and her lover, Aegisthus. Later we learn how Orestes, Agamemnon's son, avenges his father by killing Clytemnestra and Aegisthus and is in turn pursued by the Erinyes – the Furies – because he has committed matricide. But this cycle of bloodshed, violence, murder, and revenge goes back much further, to the time when Atreus, the father of Agamemnon and Menelaus, revenged himself on his brother Thyestes by killing his children and serving them up to their unsuspecting father at a banquet.

Thus the Atridae, the two sons of Atreus, bore the blood-guilt of their father, and there began the ghastly cycle of murder breeding murder, revenge breeding further revenge, through generation after generation, with the gods looking on implacably. Another cycle concerns the rulers of Thebes, in Boeotia, in which the same relentless powers that govern men's destinies impel Oedipus first to kill his father Laius, king of Thebes, and then unwittingly to marry his own mother, Jocasta. It forms the theme for Sophocles' greatest tragedy, *Oedipus Rex*.

From a strictly archaeological viewpoint, these legends have a peculiar interest. They abound in place names such as Mycenae, Thebes, Orchomenos, Tiryns, Pylos, Iolkos – all apparently the residences of Mycenaean, or as Homer terms them, Achaean royal families. And when archaeologists began to investigate these and other places with the spade, they found the actual remains of Mycenaean settlements. However, in classical Greek times (the sixth century B.C. and later) most Mycenaean cities had ceased to be of importance, the centres of power having shifted elsewhere, except in a few places such as Athens, Sparta, and Thebes.

In one sense this 'lost world' was never lost. The classical Greeks believed the stories and knew many of the cities that were their setting. They remembered these places as the homes of their ancestors, though the Mycenaeans had flourished at least seven hundred years earlier. Some had remained inhabited; others were mere ruins, the remains of buildings and of walls built of massive stone blocks, which the later Greeks called Cyclopean, believing that only the Cyclopes, who were giants, could have built them. Homer wrote of 'Tiryns of the great walls' and 'Mycenae, rich in gold'. The great walls of Tiryns are still there to be seen, and Schliemann found that Homer's description of Mycenae was confirmed by the excavations.

But long before the German archaeologist appeared on the scene, Greek and Roman visitors had seen and described Mycenae. In the second century A.D. a Greek traveller, Pausanias, visited the site and made a careful study of its topography.

> Parts of the wall are still preserved [he wrote], as well as the gate over which lions stand. These also they say are the work of the Cyclopes. ... There is a tomb of Atreus, and there are also tombs of all those whom Aegisthus murdered on their return from Troy after entertaining them at a banquet. ... Clytemnestra and Aegisthus were buried a little outside the wall, for they were not deemed worthy of burial within it, where Agamemnon lies and those who were murdered with him.

The 'gate over which lions stand', once the main entrance

to the fortified citadel, is still there. The two great sculptured beasts that are posed in confrontation, filling the pediment above the opening, once gazed down on the approaches to the gate. Their heads, which were probably of material different from the limestone figures and which were dowelled on to the necks, have long since disappeared, but the rest of the composition remains as the oldest surviving example of monumental sculpture in Greece. And it is one of the most famous. Beneath these figures and through this portal Agamemnon led his followers at the start of their expedition to lay siege to Troy.

The Cyclopean walls that girdled the fortress may also still be seen, almost in their entire length of more than half a mile. Built of huge stone blocks, each 'so large that a pair of mules could not even stir the smallest of them' (as Pausanias said of the walls of Tiryns), these great enclosing walls are in some places more than thirty feet thick. At one point, near the Lion Gate, they are built around the shaft graves where Agamemnon and those others 'deemed worthy' were said to have been interred. Schliemann, following literally Pausanias' description, ignored the tombs outside the walls and started his excavations within the citadel. He was rewarded by finding the royal shaft graves with their fabulous treasures of gold, silver, and bronze. He believed these were in fact the burial places of Agamemnon and his companions, but we now know they were dug about four hundred years before that great king was treacherously murdered.

What of the tombs built 'a little outside the wall'? We can still see them today, and they still bear the titles given them by Pausanias, such as the Treasury of Atreus and the Tomb of Clytemnestra. These renowned tholoi or beehive tombs mark a new departure in burial practices, first appearing in the fifteenth century B.C. Although they are later than the shaft graves, most of them date from a time before the Trojan War. Each of these magnificent funerary monuments is in the shape of a gigantic stone beehive, usually built into the hillside and approached by a long, stone-walled corridor called a dromos. The so-called Tomb of Aegisthus, near the Lion Gate and the Tomb of Clytemnestra, is built of unhewn stone, with a simple

Funeral masks covered the faces of some of the princes who were buried in the shaft graves at Mycenae; that shown opposite, made of gold, was one of three that were discovered in the same grave. Other offerings buried with the dead included this rock crystal bowl which represents a duck, and the gold cup (below). Probably used for libations, it has handles decorated with birds, like King Nestor's cup described in the *Iliad*; and like the Cup of Nestor, it is 'pierced with golden rivets'.

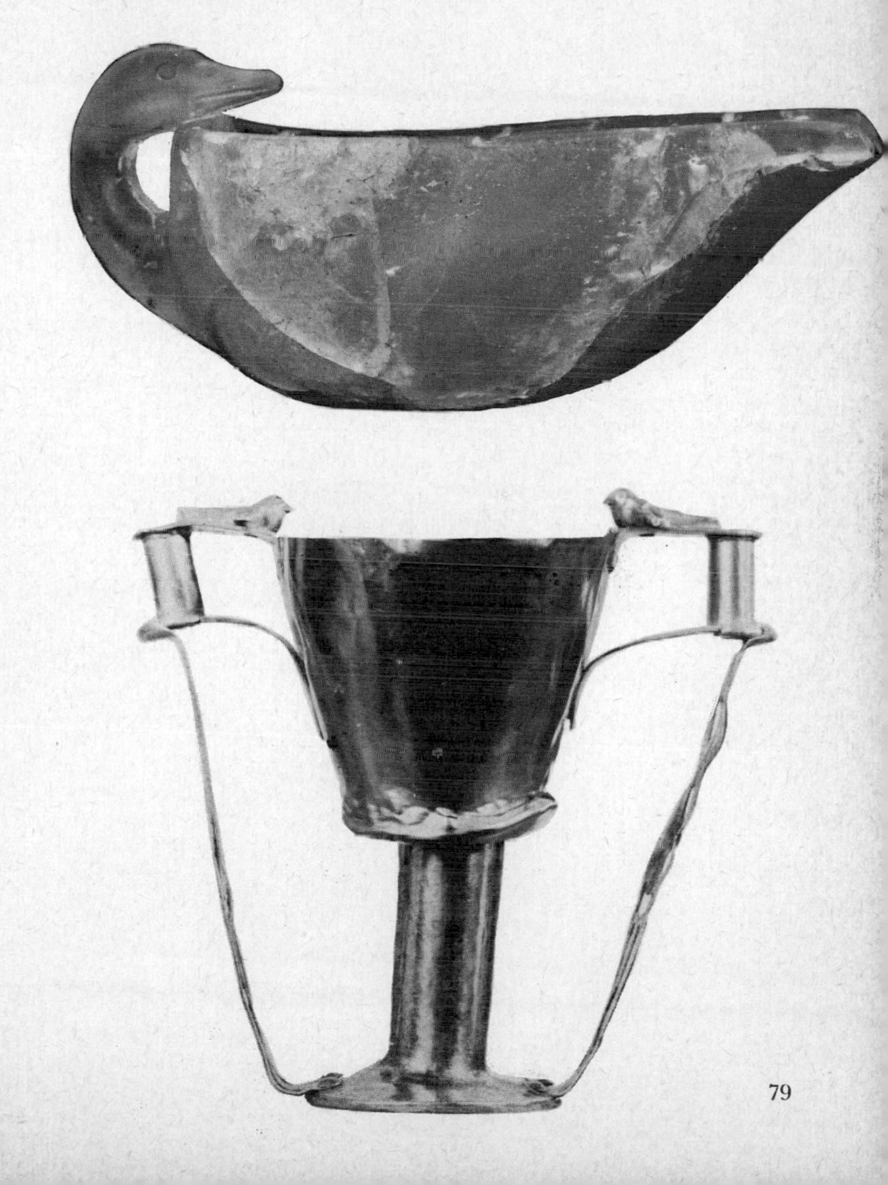

entrance, and dates from about 1450 B.C. The most majestic example is a later tholos, the Treasury of Atreus, which lies to the left of the road as one approaches Mycenae from the south. This is also sometimes called the Tomb of Agamemnon, although it was probably built before the Trojan War and may indeed have been the tomb of Atreus, father of Agamemnon.

About fifty feet in diameter at the base and almost as high from floor to apex, it is built of carefully hewn and fitted stones which rise in a perfect conical corbelled vault, the layers of masonry being graded, with the widest at the bottom and the narrowest at the top. One gets the impression that the tomb is almost twice as high as it is wide, whereas the width is actually slightly greater than the height. The massive inner lintel above the seventeen-foot-high doorway accurately curved on the inside to fit the circular tomb, weighs more than one hundred tons, a more massive building unit than any used even in the great Egyptian pyramids. The interior walls were originally studded or faced with bronze ornaments. On the exterior façade, engaged carved columns of green stone flanked the entrance. Above this opening was a decorative panel of variously coloured, carved stone, fragments of which are scattered about in half a dozen European museums. This three-thousand-year-old sepulchre is one of the architectural marvels of the ancient world.

Similar but less monumental tombs have been found at other Mycenaean sites on the mainland, and some mausoleums of this character have also been found in Crete. Most of them have long since been robbed of their contents. One or two have been found almost intact, however, with the skeletons of the royal dead lying amid the treasures that accompanied them to their graves. Such a tomb at Dendra, near Mycenae, yielded exquisitely embossed and inlaid cups of gold and silver, jewellery, weapons, and other paraphernalia, which had all belonged to members of a royal family.

Agamemnon, Achilles, Nestor, Odysseus, and other Homeric heroes belonged to a warrior race, unlike the peaceful Minoan islanders. They are legendary figures, but they represent historic personages; and it was men like them who built and lived within the frowning walls of Mycenae and Tiryns, who raided

The gold 'Mask of Agamemnon'.

far and wide by sea and land, occupying territory and ruling their subject peoples. 'I have captured twelve towns from the sea, besides eleven that I took by land', Achilles boasts in the *Iliad*. There need not necessarily have been many warriors; they could have been few in number, but formidable in strength and military skill – a warrior aristocracy, like the Normans of much later times.

The mainland of Greece, with its fortified citadels often within a very short distance of each other, as in the case of Mycenae and Tiryns, was not a unified realm, but rather an assemblage of kingdoms. The Achaean heroes were for the most part kings in their own right. Although they all seem to have owed feudal allegiance to Agamemnon, they fought against as well as alongside each other.

The kingdom of Achilles and the dominions of his father, Peleus, who was still living at the time of the Trojan War, were in Thessaly. The wide Thessalian plains are nearer to Troy and to Asia Minor than is the Peloponnesus, where Agamemnon ruled, and remote enough from the latter's stronghold to encourage the heroic spirit of independence so emphatically demonstrated by Achilles in the *Iliad*. In the last year of the siege of Troy this 'swift-footed' hero turns his wrath on his overlord, when the Mycenaean king claims the slave girl Briseis 'of the lovely cheeks', whom Achilles had won as a battle prize:

> You shameless schemer . . . always aiming at a profitable deal! How can you expect any of the men to give you loyal service when you send them on a raid or into battle? It was no quarrel with the Trojan spearmen that brought *me* here to fight. They have never done *me* any harm. They have never lifted cow or horse of mine, nor ravaged any crop that the deep soil of Phthia grows to feed her men; for the roaring seas and many a dark range of mountains lie between us.

As his anger mounts, Achilles reviles the king in more intemperate terms:

> You drunken sot . . . with the eyes of a dog and the courage of a doe! You never have the pluck to arm yourself and go into battle with the men or to join the other captains in an ambush – you would sooner die. It pays you better to stay in camp, filching the prizes of anyone

that contradicts you, and flourishing at your people's cost because they are too feeble to resist. ...

It has been plausibly suggested that the idea of glorifying Achilles at the expense of Agamemnon – a story that was given its final form in the *Iliad* – came from northern Greece. It seems hardly likely that the court poets of Mycenae would have ever ventured to recite a tale in which their great king was so thoroughly upbraided by a comrade-in-arms of whatever rank.

Mycenaean Greece had long known the impress of Minoan culture. But in view of the evidence we have discussed, scholarly opinion gradually moved away from Evans's belief that such places as Mycenae and Tiryns – fortified palaces with adjoining towns – were Minoan colonies, mere offshoots of the island civilization. Indeed, by the time of the Trojan War Crete was evidently merely another Achaean kingdom. Among the troops that assisted Agamemnon at the siege of Troy, according to the *Iliad*, was a contingent from Crete, then ruled by Idomeneus, described by Homer as a grandson of Minos. Thus Minos would himself have been an Achaean king; in fact, *Minos* may have been, or have become, a royal title rather than the name of an individual ruler.

It is widely believed that Knossos was sacked by the Mycenaeans about 1400 B.C. By that date, in any event, the mainlanders had long since learned enough about seafaring to compete with the Cretans, and over the next two centuries they developed a commercial empire that virtually monopolized the sea-borne trade in the Aegean and in other areas of the Mediterranean. Mycenaean pottery, obviously produced in large quantities to satisfy widely distributed markets, has been found at sites far up the Nile, in Sicily and along the shore of the Bay of Naples, and in Macedonia and at Troy, as well as in Syria and Palestine. To implement this foreign commerce Mycenaean trading stations and settlements took root and flourished on the islands of Rhodes and Cyprus, on the western shores of Asia Minor and the Levant, and elsewhere. We might gather from the records that Rhodes enjoyed an almost independent status, as it was firmly enough established as an outpost of Mycenaean authority to bring the great king of the Hittites to civil terms in the course of a dispute.

All that has been said thus far about the Mycenaeans has been gleaned from archaeological evidence, plus some contemporary documents of other civilizations, and the later epics of Homer. When Evans first began excavating the remains at Knossos he thought they were the ruins of Mycenaean buildings. He also believed that such a highly civilized society would have had to rely upon a system of writing for its bookkeeping and administration. Eventually he recognized Knossos for what it was – a monument of Minoan culture, which was revealed in ever greater detail as his investigations progressed.

The reliefs on the gold Vaphio cups represent the capture of two wild bulls, to provide animals for the Cretan bull games or to keep the beasts from roaming free about a herd of cattle. On this cup, a trapped bull struggles to liberate himself. The other illustrations are details from the matching cup; a bull is being decoyed by a cow; and a herdsman hobbles his leg with a rope.

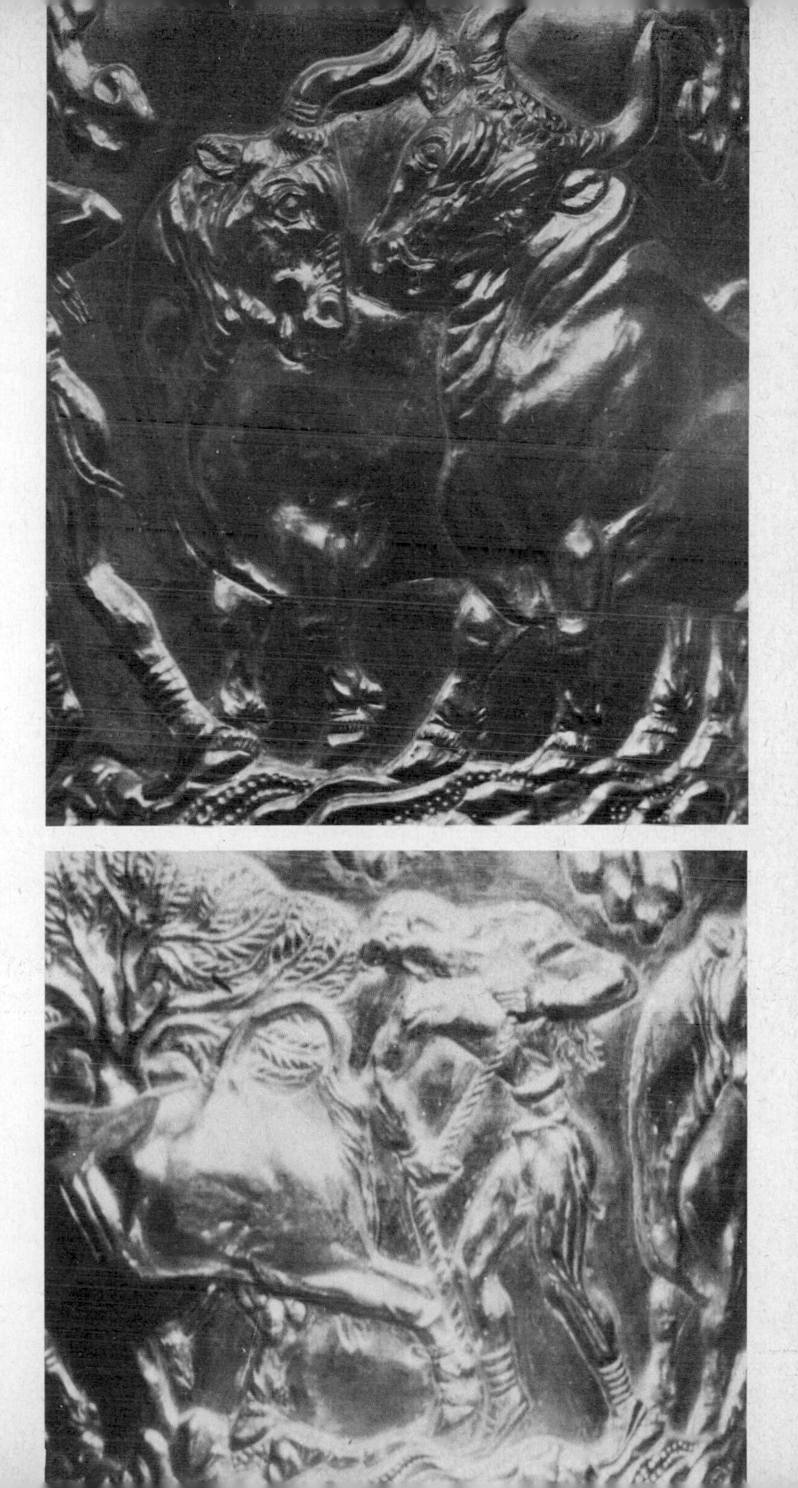

The Warrior Vase shows a file of six helmeted Mycenaean soldiers carrying round shields and lances.

Also, he discovered evidence of three writing systems, one a form of hieroglyphics, and the others the so-called Linear A and Linear B scripts, but none of them had been deciphered at the time of his death in 1941.

Then, in 1952, a discovery was made that added an entirely new dimension to the understanding of Mycenaean civilization. A brilliant young English architect, Michael Ventris, announced that he believed he had 'cracked' the Linear B script and that it represented an early form of the Greek language. For the first time it could be *proved* that the Mycenaeans were Greek; and now they would be allowed to speak for themselves. This was perhaps the greatest feat of decipherment ever achieved, even more remarkable than the decipherments of Egyptian hieroglyphs by Champollion and of cuneiform by Rawlinson and others. For unlike these earlier men, Ventris had no bilingual clues to guide him; no one has yet found identical texts written both in Linear B and in a previously known script.

It had taken Ventris sixteen years – ever since as a schoolboy he had heard Evans lecture – to break this most difficult of 'codes'; for years he had been in communication with other scholars working on the same problem. They exchanged data, and as new material was published or discovered it was studied, analysed, and compared. At first Ventris had to rely only on the tablets discovered by Evans at Knossos, few of which – one hundred and sixty or so out of a total of about three thousand – had been published.

In 1939 Carl Blegen of the University of Cincinnati had begun to excavate at Pylos, in the south-western Peloponnesus, and found a Mycenaean palace, which he and many archaeologists believe to have been that of the sage King Nestor, wise counsellor and friend of the other Achaean leaders. In the palace archives Blegen came upon numerous clay tablets that had been baked (and thus accidentally preserved) in the fire that destroyed Pylos towards the end of the thirteenth century B.C. These too were written in the Linear B script. The publication of these in 1951 further advanced Ventris's work. Still later more tablets turned up at Mycenae, also in the now familiar Linear B script. Then, in 1952, Sir John Myres published in the second volume of *Scripta Minoa* the tablets that Evans had found, and that same year Blegen found more tablets at Pylos.

With all this virgin material, Ventris and his colleagues, especially his friend and collaborator John Chadwick, were able to test the theory that forced itself on Ventris – that the documents were in some form of Greek. Up till 1952 he had assumed, with others, that they were written in some non-Greek language, a language possibly related to Etruscan; but after laborious grammatical analyses and comparative studies, he found that some tablets contained Cretan place-names, such as Knossos, Phaistos, and Tylissos; the grammatical structure of the language – as shown, for instance, in variant word-endings – was like that of Greek, but a relatively early form of the language, which seemed to bear some faint similarity to that of Homer.

Ventris was essentially a modest man, generous, open-hearted, with no scholarly axe to grind (he was not a professional philologist), and it was not until he and Chadwick had tested their theory to the full and discussed it with other researchers that they published their historic work, *Documents in Mycenaean Greek*. They had conquered, as one writer happily expressed it, 'the Everest of Greek archaeology'. Shortly before the publication of the book Ventris met a tragic death in a road accident; he was thirty-four years old.

Today the majority of Greek scholars, as well as specialists in Aegean archaeology, accept Ventris's decipherment, although the documents are still not easy to read and some of Ventris's conclusions may have to be modified in the light of further research. Also there are a few scholars, and eminent ones, who have yet to be convinced that the language is in fact Greek. But assuming that the majority are right, this astonishing revelation poses an entirely new set of problems. For if the Linear B tablets found at Knossos (and they have been found nowhere else on the island) are in Greek, and if their dating of about 1400 B.C. is accepted, it means that Greek-speaking people must have been ruling at Knossos in the fifteenth century B.C. And if the Mycenaeans were at Knossos in 1400 B.C., then it can hardly have been they who destroyed the palaces at about this time. When had they come from the mainland? How long had they been on the island?

Tablets written in Linear A, as well as in an earlier hieroglyphic version of it, have been found throughout the island of Crete but nowhere else. The Linear A form apparently replaced the hieroglyphs around 1750 B.C., remained in use for some three centuries, and then gave way to Linear B. It became clear that the last was an adaptation of the Minoan script and was used to give written form to the Greek language. It uses similar symbols, but in a different way – not unlike the differences between the Greek and Roman alphabets, as Chadwick has pointed out.

The documents themselves are disappointing in that they include no literature, only lists and inventories, records kept by the palace clerks. These, however, provide fascinating details concerning the equipment and organization of Mycenaean life. Many refer to objects such as swords, tripods, chariots. A

This golden octopus was used as a dress ornament. Octopuses were a frequent decorative device in Aegean art; this one is novel, however, in having only seven tentacles.

typical example, found in the Knossian armoury, can be translated into English by the Ventris system: 'Horse (chariots), painted crimson and with joinery work complete, supplied with reins. The bridle (?) is of leather, with fittings (?) of horn, and there is (no?) "heel" (?).' Another series of tablets from Knossos, a muster roll, refers to an armoured brigade, which in Chadwick's estimation may have comprised a force of well over a hundred chariots.

Other tablets describe furnishings in a surprising variety of specialized forms – chairs, footstools, tables, fire tools, and the like – many of which would appear to have been elaborately wrought and which reflect an intricate domestic economy. Chairs, for instance, were made of ebony and ornamented with delicately carved and inlaid ivory; tables were of marble inlaid with rock crystal, gold, and ivory. And to give tangible evidence to this record of luxury and convenience, in 1955 Blegen found in the palace at Pylos a built-in bath with a place for a sponge.

The list of specialized workmen and craftsmen drawn from the inscriptions reveals a complex and highly organized society. There were seamstresses and cleaners, saddle makers or leather workers, carpenters and masons, shipbuilders and caulkers, bronzesmiths and goldsmiths, bowmakers and, of course, potters, and so on down a long line of trades and occupations, including a variety of agricultural pursuits. That there were also slave traders is indicated by the number of captive peoples, many of whom seem to have been brought from the west coast of Asia Minor, and who performed menial chores in the palaces and great houses.

There are no Mycenaean inscriptions such as those found in Egypt and Mesopotamia that proclaim the might and right of rulers and the omnipotence of the gods. Still other tablets, however, refer to people who appear to have well-known Homeric names, such as Hector, while on three tablets discovered at Pylos appear the names of several familiar Greek gods – Poseidon, Zeus, Hera, Athena, Hermes, and others. There is also, at Pylos and at Knossos, a frequent reference to *Potnia* – 'Mistress' or 'Our Lady'; these last inscriptions confirm what archaeologists had long suspected from the evidence on seals discovered on the mainland – that the Mycenaeans also worshipped the Minoan mother goddess.

The inscriptions give evidence of filing systems that maintained records of land, food supplies, and slaves – some called 'servants of the god' and others belonging to the king. The impression one gets is of a tightly organized bureaucracy, with many scribes keeping records of land tenure, military supplies, taxation, heads of sheep, cattle, and other domesticated beasts, amounts of oil, wine, and grain, and so on. In many respects it seems quite unlike the much simpler society that Homer describes.

It is quite possible that the Minoans, and even the Mycenaeans, also wrote on papyrus, which they could have imported from Egypt, and there is a tradition of writing on palm leaves, leather, and bark. But such documents would naturally have perished; none have been found, and it is disappointing that no document in either Linear A or B has to date turned up in Egypt.

Recently the philologist Leonard Palmer has ventured a theory that the tablets found at Knossos date no earlier than 1200 B.C.; that the palace there did not go into a decline after 1400 B.C.; and that it was during the two centuries of Achaean domination between those dates that Knossos actually reached its full glory. Even the famous frescoes, including those of the bull-leapers, might belong to this epoch, according to Palmer's contention. His theory cannot be discussed here in any detail; it can only be put on record with the comment that many archaeologists disagree with it. If he were to be proved right the destruction of Knossos could have occurred about the same time as the mainland palaces were destroyed. It would also follow that Homer could have been right in stating that at Agamemnon's behest, Crete was able to contribute a large expeditionary force to the Mycenaean cause at Troy.

> The illustrious spearman Idomeneus led the Cretans [the *Iliad* reports]; the men from Knossos, from Gortyn of the Great Walls, from Lyktos, Miletus, chalky Lykastos, Phaistos, and Rhytion, fine cities all of them; and the other troops that had their homes in Crete of the Hundred Towns. All these were led by the great spearman Idomeneus and by Meriones, a compeer of the man-destroying war god. Eighty black ships came under their command.

Despite Palmer's contention, however, it is widely believed that Evans was right and that Knossos was laid waste about 1400 B.C., not later.

At the end of the thirteenth century B.C., the great Mycenaean palaces, such as Tiryns, Pylos, and Iolkos, were burned level, never to rise again. Again and again, in examining these sites, one sees the sinister marks of fire. Iolkos, the legendary home of Jason in Thessaly, is the most mouth-watering archaeological site in Greece. This ancient city was not built high on rock, but on low-lying ground near the harbour. Successive rebuildings have produced a tell – that is, a mound created by many centuries of almost continuous occupation and repeated rebuilding – with clearly stratified layers that range from a possible early level of about 2300 B.C. down through the entire Bronze Age – including, of course, the Mycenaean period (roughly from 1600 to 1200 B.C.) – to the eighth century B.C. The marks of burning are clearly visible in the side of the mound. The late Alan Wace, who found Linear B tablets at Mycenae, thought there might be a possibility of finding palace archives amid the debris at Iolkos, tablets baked by fire to an enduring hardness. (The tablets were never deliberately fired.) One hopes he was right; time alone will show. Part of the modern town of Volos sits on top of the mound, however, and would have to be demolished before the site could be thoroughly explored.

At Tiryns the evidence is even more dramatic, for there, buried beneath charred debris at the foot of the city walls, lay the skeletons of the last defenders where they fell or where their bodies were thrown. Among the tablets found by Blegen at Pylos, tablets whose preservation is due to the fire that destroyed the palace, are some that appear to suggest preparations for defence against an impending attack. Watchers are posted to guard the coast; ships' crews – 'rowers' – are dispatched on naval business, significantly to a point where there were no coastal forts. At Mycenae, as elsewhere, excavations have revealed that defences were strengthened and the water supply was protected. At Gla, on Lake Copais in Boeotia, not far from Thebes, a huge wall was built – the longest defence-work ever erected in Mycenaean Greece. Its ruins were discovered in a shattered condition; it may never have been finished. In any event, the settlement it was supposed to guard perished shortly after it was first occupied. There are no written records of this catastrophe. Only the mute stones stand witness to whatever events took place.

According to legend and tradition, the last wave of invading Greeks were the descendants of Heracles – the Heraclidae – who, meeting resistance when they returned to the Peloponnesus, conquered the land by force. To historians this is known as the invasion of the Dorians, an illiterate people who drove down from somewhere in the north-western regions, passing through central Greece and occupying much of the Peloponnesus by the twelfth century B.C. In the words of Blegen:

> The Dorian invasion, whatever its sources and however it ran its course, has left a broad gash, like a fire-scar in a mountain forest, cutting through the archaeological panorama of ancient Greek history. Many towns that flourished in the preceding Heroic Age were henceforth abandoned or declined to a state of insignificance. Even some of the great ... strongholds sank into virtual oblivion, and the places where they had stood were lost from the view of men.

It was roughly about this time (the twelfth century B.C.) that hordes of migrants were pouring down the coast of Syria and Palestine and on to Egypt, where they were met and defeated by Ramesses III. Shortly before, the great Hittite empire in Anatolia had collapsed under the weight of hosts of invaders. There seems to have been a great stirring of peoples, tribe thrusting out tribe, each fighting for new lands. Aside from the Egyptian documents and monuments, the written records tell us little of all this; only occasionally, as in Homer, does one get a clue as to what was happening. The Trojan War, allegedly fought to avenge the honour of Menelaus, in fact may have represented a desperate attempt by the Mycenaeans – or Achaeans, as Homer calls them – to secure new lands and to control the trade routes that led to the north and to the east.

When the Mycenaean heroes won their war against Troy, they returned home, leaving no settlers at the site. But their descendants, fleeing from the domination of their Dorian overlords, eventually did settle in Asia, primarily on the coast south of Troy and on the islands near by. One great Mycenaean city, Athens, had escaped destruction by the Dorian hordes, and it was into Athens that the Mycenaean refugees first fled before they crossed the Aegean to the new land, which came to be called Ionia. This migration from the mainland centres continued throughout the Dark Age of Greece.

The refugees brought with them an ancient tradition of song. An Ionian elegy written in the seventh century B.C. recalls the foundation of the city of Colophon centuries before by men who had fled from the Peloponnesus.

> We left Pylos, the town of Neleus, and reached lovely Asia by sea.
> We settled in fair Colophon, in the strength of our might. . . .

Neleus had been the father of King Nestor and the founder of the town of Pylos. About a century after the Trojan War, his heirs, seeking new lands, led a band of migrants across the seas from Greece to Ionia. There the Mycenaean refugees had to fight to dislodge the native inhabitants; like their forefathers, the warriors of the *Iliad*, they found themselves battling in a hostile land along the coast of Asia. When their descendants in Ionia sang of the ventures of those remote Mycenaean heroes who had fought at Troy, it might have recalled to them as well the struggles that had secured a homeland for them in Ionia.

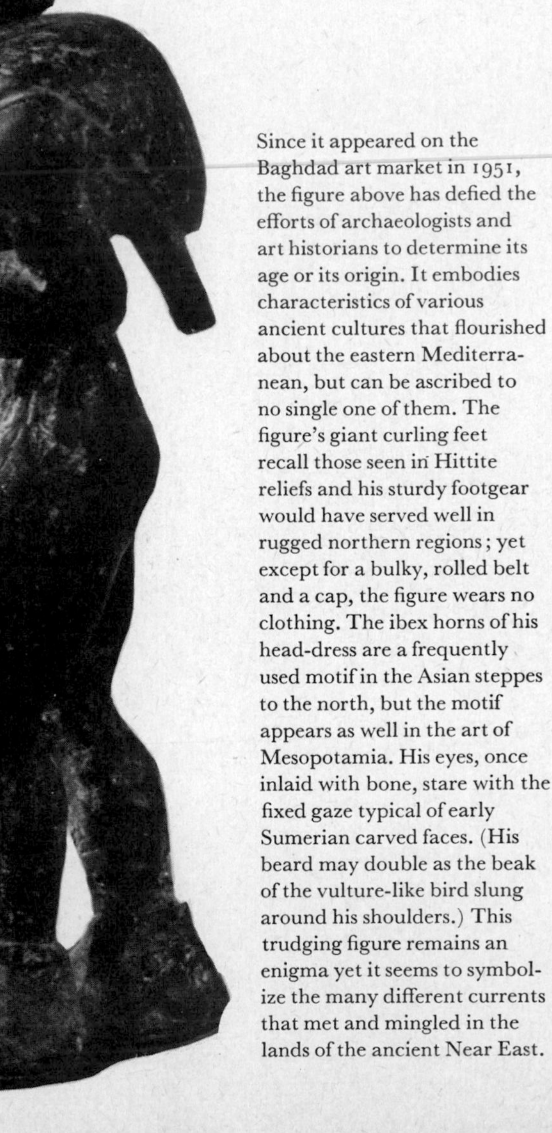

Since it appeared on the Baghdad art market in 1951, the figure above has defied the efforts of archaeologists and art historians to determine its age or its origin. It embodies characteristics of various ancient cultures that flourished about the eastern Mediterranean, but can be ascribed to no single one of them. The figure's giant curling feet recall those seen in Hittite reliefs and his sturdy footgear would have served well in rugged northern regions; yet except for a bulky, rolled belt and a cap, the figure wears no clothing. The ibex horns of his head-dress are a frequently used motif in the Asian steppes to the north, but the motif appears as well in the art of Mesopotamia. His eyes, once inlaid with bone, stare with the fixed gaze typical of early Sumerian carved faces. (His beard may double as the beak of the vulture-like bird slung around his shoulders.) This trudging figure remains an enigma yet it seems to symbolize the many different currents that met and mingled in the lands of the ancient Near East.

3 The Lost Worlds of Anatolia

Anatolia was the home of the Hittites, who between three and four thousand years ago ranked as one of the great civilized powers of the ancient world. One glance at a map of Turkey will show the geographical reasons why the peninsula of Asia Minor was so important in ancient times. The shape of the country roughly resembles the head of an Assyrian lion, the shoulders of which are firmly set in Asia, the crown of the skull supporting the Black Sea, the mane overhanging the east Mediterranean and Cyprus, while the nose thrusts out boldly into the Aegean, linking Asia with eastern Europe. To change the metaphor, Anatolia is an enormous two-way land bridge between Europe and Asia, the route by which the Mycenaeans may have entered Greece and by which Alexander invaded Asia.

Few areas of comparable size anywhere in the world present such a variety of climates and landscapes. The western coast, fronting the Aegean, is typically Mediterranean, hardly distinguishable from the coast of southern Greece and the Cyclades. There are olive groves and vineyards; the climate is warm and relaxing, with dry summers and rainy winters. The southern

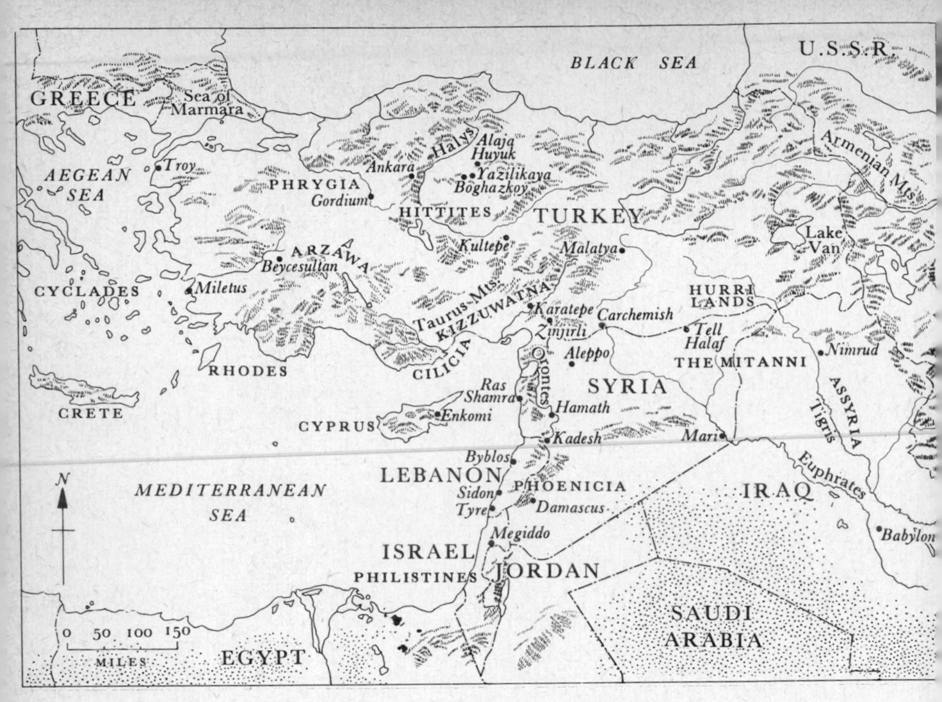

Anatolia.

coast, overlooking Cyprus, grows cotton and citrus fruit. Much of the Black Sea coast is semi-tropical, whereas the eastern mountains have an alpine climate. Someone has commented that a Swiss, a Scotsman, an Italian, a Russian, and an African would each find some part of Asia Minor where he would feel comfortable.

However, the mountainous character of much of the country is more significant to the story of Anatolia than these climatic variations. The mountains of the Taurus range loom so enormously that they seemed to divide the eastern Mediterranean world into northern and southern halves; even to the imperial Roman legions looking north from the Syrian plains they constituted an almost impassable barrier. Parts of central Anatolia are like a raging sea turned to stone; peaks and massifs rear up on every side, tumbling to the restless horizon. From the central plateau, where the Hittites lived, one looks eastward towards the towering peak of Erjiyes Dagh, almost thirteen thousand feet high and snow-capped. Beyond it the chain of the Anti-Taurus runs north-eastwards to merge with the highlands of

Armenia. This violent landscape, fit home for mysterious gods and peoples, is utterly unlike the monotonous plains of the Tigris and Euphrates or the Indus, or the well-nurtured valley of the Nile.

The people who have lived in Asia Minor during the past seven thousand years have consequently differed widely in character. There would be little in common between, say, a Cilician living in the warm south-east and a man living near the Pontus, on the Black Sea; and even less between them and someone living on the high central plateau or a person dwelling near the shores of 'windy Troy'.

Anatolia remains the least-known sector of that part of the world which nourished the earliest civilizations. For some five hundred years it was the heartland of the Ottoman Empire, a closed-in territory that few Europeans were allowed to penetrate. Even after the rebellion under Ataturk, when unbelievers were shown greater tolerance, poor communications and other factors still militated against visits from foreigners. Greece has attracted tourists since the Renaissance and even before – indeed since Roman days. Egypt has had a tourist industry for more than fifty years. Even Babylonia has for some time been reasonably accessible to foreign scholars, although it offers few attractions to tourists. But Anatolia has remained apart until quite recently.

Perhaps this is just as well, since it may have saved archaeologically valuable remains from the ignorant, indiscriminate plundering that destroyed so much in Egypt and Mesopotamia, preserving them against a time when modern, scientific techniques would extract the maximum information from such undisturbed sites as still remain.

The discovery of the lost world of the Hittites and their neighbours vies with that of Sumer and of Crete as a fascinating archaeological story, the end of which is not yet in sight. In the case of Mesopotamia and Anatolia investigators were led first by biblical reference (though in the latter case supplemented by Egyptian and Assyrian inscriptions). But the search was confused by the fact that the Hittites of the Bible, who occupied parts of Syria, were not the Hittites who had earlier fought the Egyptians at Kadesh. The trail led the hunters by a devious route, with many doublings and some blind alleys, from an inscribed stone on the wall of a mosque in Aleppo to obscure passages in the Book of Numbers, from Egyptian temple inscriptions and the files of Akhenaten's diplomatic correspondence to the cuneiform records of the early Assyrian kings, from the plains of Syria to beyond the mighty mountains of the Taurus.

In a sense those who have read thus far in these books are in a position similar to that of scholars of half a century ago. Like them, the reader possesses certain evidence, to which more will be added in the following pages. They know, of course, about the ancient Egyptians and are aware that for a while during the New Kingdom the Hittites were among the Egyptians' most deadly foes. They know that contemporaneously with Egypt Mesopotamia had produced a succession of civilizations – Sumerian, Akkadian, Babylonian, Assyrian – and that these people wrote in cuneiform on clay tablets. They know that the horse and chariot were introduced into Egypt about 1600 B.C.

Sea Peoples in crested helmets fight the Egyptians. From the pictorial records of Ramesses III.

and appeared in Greece at about the same time; the Mycenaeans, Homer's 'bronze-clad Achaeans', were adept with this military weapon. And they will also recall that from about 2000 to 1700 B.C. there was a movement of Indo-European peoples into Greece, perhaps via Asia Minor, and later into the Indus Valley via Afghanistan. In 1280 B.C. the pharaoh Ramesses II signed a treaty of friendship with the Hittite king Hattusilis III, and ninety-three years later Ramesses III defeated a coalition of invaders who, forging down the coast of Syria and Palestine, had reached the very gates of Egypt. Among these Peoples of the Sea, as we have come to call them, were those the Egyptians named the Danuna, whom some identify as Homer's Danaoi.

Syria and Palestine, not having nurtured a major civilization up to this point in the history of the ancient world, have hardly been mentioned in the previous pages, but it is worth recalling that among the best known of the Old Testament stories is that of King David and Uriah the Hittite, whose wife David coveted; and that in the Book of Numbers it is stated that, 'The Amalekites dwell in the land of the south; and the Hittites, and the Jebusites, and the Amorites dwell in the mountains [of Syria].' Also, in the Second Book of Kings, when the Assyrians were besieging Samaria, the Samarians quote them as saying, 'Lo, the king of Israel hath hired against us the king of the Hittites.'

The statements in the foregoing paragraph may seem like a bewildering catalogue of unrelated information. They provide, however, vital clues that helped archaeologists and scholars in other fields to establish the identity of the Hittites and to retrace the complex ancient history of Anatolia. With them in mind we also can thread our way through this labyrinth of the past.

In one form or another the name of the Hittites kept cropping up again and again. In Egypt Ramesses II left huge temple reliefs illustrating and describing his battles with the 'abominable Kheta', as he once termed the Hittites when they were his enemies. We see the pharaoh in his war chariot shooting arrows into the foe, and the panic-stricken Hittite soldiers, men with long noses and prognathous jaws, falling headlong into the Orontes River, near the Syrian town where the battle was fought. (As we have earlier noted, the battle was actually a stand-off; the Hittites were by no means beaten in this conflict.) Again, in Mesopotamia an inscription dating from the reign of the Assyrian king Tiglath-pileser I (1100 B.C.) described how that ruler came into contact with a powerful kingdom called Great Hatti; and how later, returning from a campaign, Tiglath-pileser received homage from another king of Great Hatti. The Hittites of the Hebrews, the Kheta of the Egyptians, and the Hatti of the Assyrians, it was assumed, were all the same people. But who were they? And where did they come from? Had they a capital city, and if so, where was it?

As in Sumer and as in Crete, it was the discovery of a hitherto-unknown form of writing which first put archaeologists on the scent. In 1812 an explorer named Johann Burckhardt came upon an inscribed block of basalt at Hamath, in Syria. No one else took much notice of the discovery at the time. Later, in 1871, a similar block was found in the wall of a mosque in Aleppo. Both bore inscriptions in a form of hieroglyphic writing which resembled no known language. The worshippers at the mosque considered the stone holy, and resented any attempt by foreigners to examine it. However, copies were made and circulated, but linguists could make nothing of them. Following Burckhardt's discovery, several decades were to pass before reports began to filter through that what appeared to be similar hieroglyphs had been found engraved on rocks high in the Taurus mountains, hundreds of miles to the north.

A. H. Sayce, a well-known Assyriologist, announced in 1876 that he believed both the Hamath and Aleppo inscriptions to be in the Hittite language, and in subsequent articles he also tentatively identified rock inscriptions at Ivriz, Boghazkoy, and Alaja Huyuk as being in Hittite. These and other sites had been visited by a number of adventurous travellers between 1834 and 1876. From the end of the eighteenth century on, more and more explorers mounted expeditions into what was still the dangerous hinterland of Anatolia. The country was difficult to travel in and at the time extremely inhospitable.

Ramesses II's version of a battle with the Hittites.

Excitement grew as each explorer brought back reports of inscriptions, sculptures, and even the ruins of cities, high up in the central tableland of Anatolia.

Of such ruins the most impressive were found near Boghazkoy, an obscure village high in the mountains within the bend of the Halys River, and another at Alaja Huyuk, fifteen miles to the north-east. Here were not only inscriptions in the mysterious writing first found at Hamath, but great sculptured reliefs depicting men of somewhat similar appearance to the Kheta shown on the ancient Egyptian temple reliefs. Had the archaeologists traced the elusive Hittites to their homeland? It seemed probable, yet while the writing system remained undeciphered it could not be proved. The final investigation, which had only just begun, was to show that the Hittites were relative latecomers to Asia Minor, which had known other rich and highly developed cultures long before their time. But this is to anticipate.

In 1887 another clue turned up in far-off Egypt. It was found not by an archaeologist, but by an Egyptian peasant woman digging for *sebakh* at el Amarna, Pharaoh Akhenaten's long-deserted capital. (*Sebakh* is the name given to the crumbled mud brick of ancient cities, which the practical Arabs discovered makes a useful fertilizer.) The woman came upon large quantities of baked-clay tablets, which were eventually loaded into a sack and carried to the nearest dealer (many of them crumbled to dust during their rough passage.) The dealer recognized that the tablets bore cuneiform inscriptions, but at first officials refused to believe that these were genuine. By the time the authenticity of the tablets had been established many of them had been destroyed. Among those which remained, however, were a series of letters addressed in the Akkadian language to the pharaoh by certain of his Syrian and Palestinian vassals and city governors. With this correspondence was the famous appeal from Ribbadi, quoted in volume one.

There were also two letters written in an unknown language, though the word Arzawa could be made out. A Norwegian scholar suggested that one of these was from the pharaoh Amenhotep III to the king of a state called Arzawa (wherever that might be) and that the other was probably written from Arzawa to Egypt. He believed that the language belonged to the Indo-European linguistic group. The theory attracted little attention, although one fact was clear. The peasant woman had come upon a file from Akhenaten's foreign office; some of these letters were an attempt to bring home to the pharaoh the imminent threat to his Syrian dominions by a powerful foe from the north – and the enemy that was menacing Egypt was the Kheta.

Even so this discovery did little but add to the archaeologists' frustration. They already knew that the Hittites had existed; there was abundant testimony from the peoples of lands such as Egypt and Assyria. They had even found what they strongly suspected to be the actual homeland of these people. But the Kheta themselves, if that is whom the rock-cut sculptures represented, remained silent, looking down from their niches in the Anatolian mountains – stocky, hook-nosed men in conical hats, thick woollen robes, and mountaineer's boots, surrounded by tantalizing inscriptions in hieroglyphic that no one could read.

'The day the import of your tablet was made known to me, I provided your agents with three minas of silver for the purchase of lead. Now, if you are still my brother, let me have my money by courier.' So wrote an Assyrian, probably in Assur, to one of his countrymen who was living in the thriving Assyrian trading colony outside Kultepe, a pre-Hittite settlement in central Anatolia. Their four-thousand-year-old transactions were recorded in cuneiform on clay tablets and inserted into seal-impressed clay envelopes [above].

In 1880 certain cuneiform tablets had appeared in the hands of antique dealers in Ankara, Turkey. These were the first tablets to turn up in Anatolia and had been found by peasants at a mound of ruins known as Kultepe. They were in Assyrian and proved to be valuable, but they provided meagre information about the Hittites. In 1893-4 tablets were excavated at Boghazkoy, the ancient Hattusas. These were in the same cuneiform script as the two Arzawa letters found at el Amarna, which had not yet been deciphered. A German scholar, Hugo Winckler, with the express purpose of searching for more tablets, undertook excavation at Boghazkoy. He started digging at the site in 1906.

One approaches this remote village across a wide fertile valley, but gradually the hills close in until a point is reached at which two small streams break into the plain through narrow clefts in the mountains. The gorge is deep and impressive, with steep cliffs at the sides. At the junction of the streams is the little Turkish village, consisting of but a handful of modest houses, stores, farms, and beyond them rough tracks threading the fields. Above that cluster of buildings rise the ruins of an ancient city. One sees remains of Cyclopean walls girdling a total area of some three hundred acres. Monumental gateways pierce the wall. Flanking one gateway, sculptured lions seem to roar defiance at the approaching stranger; on another, when Winckler saw it, the vigorously sculptured figure of a god strode resolutely forward, right hand clasping a battle-axe, left hand clenched, powerful muscles rippling in thigh and arm. There are power and virility in these weather-worn stone carvings, and the figures seem to shout, 'Look at us. We ruled an empire once!' Below, in the valley, the gentle murmur of the streams sounds mournfully among the rocks.

This is what Winckler saw fifty-odd years ago. Near by, he also saw the mysterious shrine of Yazilikaya, where ranks of sculptured figures, each in his tall helmet, short tunic, and boots with upturned toes, march in procession. At the centre a god and goddess confront each other. Within a secluded sanctuary another relief, carved from the living rock, shows a king embraced by a god in a tall, conical head-dress. In a niche near by the strange hieroglyphs that had baffled Sayce

Gateway at Hattusas, now called Boghazkoy.

and others still mocked the German scholar. But Winckler had not come to marvel at these sculptures, which were now well known among archaeologists. He had come to search for more tablets. He turned his attention to the area enclosed by the great walls, and made a wide trench to the top of the citadel mound.

To his astonishment and delight he came upon what had evidently been a palace archive. Over ten thousand tablets were discovered, all in cuneiform, including many in the mysterious language still referred to at that time as Arzawa. But besides the Arzawan tablets there were some in Akkadian, which could of course be read. Had he discovered the capital city of Arzawa or something different? The find would be of even greater interest if this were possibly the capital city of the long-sought-for Hittites.

It was true. This heap of stones on a rugged Turkish hillside had once been Hattusas, capital of the Hittite empire – capital

Figure guarding a gateway
at Hattusas.

At Yazilikaya is this vast, rock-cut processional scene.

of a power that, for a brief period at least, could meet even mighty Egypt on equal terms. The tablets in Akkadian revealed much. More interesting was that the tablets, written in what had been called Arzawan, were in fact in the Hittite language – that is to say, in a cuneiform script adapted to the Hittite language. When these were deciphered, largely by the Czech scholar Bedrich Hrozny, it became possible to learn something of Hittite life and culture. There were the names of successive Hittite rulers and chronicles of their conquests. There were legal documents, a code of law, correspondence with foreign rulers, even a copy (in Hittite) of the famous treaty between Ramesses II and the Hittite king Hattusilis III, of which another copy was inscribed on one of the Egyptian temples at Karnak. There was a religious literature, with hymns and rituals, and there were references to the peoples of Syria and Mesopotamia, and other peoples of Anatolia with whom the Hittites had been in contact.

After Winckler's discoveries the search was on for more tablets. Anatolia became an archaeological Mecca. Other Hittite sites were systematically explored, including Kultepe, where some tablets had earlier been found and where Winckler had dug. He had worked there for eight days but found very little. Yet, year after year, more tablets came on the market that could be traced back to this site. Eventually a

Travelling Asian metalworkers entering Egypt with their families.

Czechoslovak expedition led by Hrozny made a serious and determined effort to locate the source of these documents.

For a long time this team searched unavailingly in the main mound, while the innocent-seeming villagers, who knew very well where the tablets lay, watched with interest and made misleading suggestions. The villagers had, in fact, come upon the cache of tablets some years earlier and had been discreetly and profitably leaking them on to the market a few at a time. They had already watched two other expeditions vainly searching, but this time they were unlucky. Two of Hrozny's men were from the area and by questioning them he eventually was able to locate the true site, only a few hundred yards from the major mound, Kultepe. It yielded more than a thousand tablets, some in Assyro-Babylonian cuneiform, that revealed much about this ancient site.

Kultepe had controlled the trade route from central Anatolia down to northern Syria, and here Hrozny found the remains of a trading post in which Assyrian merchants had lived for generations before the rise of the Hittite empire. There were their neat houses and orderly offices, containing baked-clay tablets neatly stacked on shelves: bills of sale, contracts, receipts, accounts – all the paraphernalia of a prosperous trading community which lived in amity with the rulers of the near-by Bronze Age city. These merchants supervised the donkey caravans that moved between Anatolia and Assyria, exchanging Anatolian metals for the woollens and other textiles of the Tigris-Euphrates Valley.

King Tudhaliyas is shown protected by the god Sharma at Yazilikaya.

Meanwhile other sites had been identified in northern Syria, where Hittite influence was apparent, such as Carchemish, on the upper Euphrates, Milid, the modern Malatya, and Hamath. A few years before the outbreak of the First World War, a British archaeologist began to excavate at Carchemish, assisted by a young Oxford graduate named T. E. Lawrence, later to become 'Lawrence of Arabia'. They found substantial remains of a powerful city, including a great wall of sculptures with a procession of deities and warriors celebrating some great victory.

A German expedition dug at Zinjirli, and French archaeologists at Arslantepe. Other sites, such as Sakjegozu, also yielded valuable evidence – well-planned cities with temples and palaces, and ponderous but crude works of sculpture which seemed to owe something to Assyria, yet were not Assyrian. Were these Hittite remains? Most of these north Syrian sites belonged to a period considerably after 1500 B.C. There was a clear relationship between them and the mountain strongholds in Asia Minor – which were believed to be earlier – yet they were different. The solution of this mystery came later, after other significant finds.

Much was still to be learned about pre-Hittite Anatolia. Until fairly recently it was thought that human beings had not begun to occupy Anatolia much before 3000 B.C. But as a result of numerous excavations there is now considerable evidence of human occupation, in southern and south-western Asia Minor, as far back as 5000 B.C., almost three thousand years before the first evidence of Hittite occupation. Remains of villages have been discovered dating from the Neolithic and Chalcolithic Periods. But the oldest known city to have been systematically excavated is Troy, near the Dardanelles, first dug by Schliemann over ninety years ago, and subsequently re-dug more scientifically by Carl Blegen of the University of Cincinnati. The 'great' period of Troy comes in Level II, about 2400 B.C., when Troy had a monumental fortress with mansions and a high civilization with a rich and sophisticated art. The celebrated jewellery that Schliemann found, which he romantically named the Treasure of Priam, actually dates from the Early Bronze Age, over a thousand years before the traditional date of the Trojan War. Again and again the archaeologists have found at Troy the marks of fierce fire – calcined stone, vitrified bricks, and the marks of charred timber. Such a strategic position, astride the trade routes, was bound to invite attack by ambitious peoples; there were many sackings of Troy.

Not long ago, at Dorak, near the Sea of Marmara, archaeologists came upon a rich Bronze Age burial that appears to be related stylistically to Troy II, although the finds have not yet been adequately published. The graves were of a local ruler and his wife, buried in the same tomb, while near by lay another separate tomb containing one male body, probably of another king. The king entombed with his wife was accompanied by his favourite hunting dog, food offerings, and beautifully made ceremonial weapons. These, it has been reported, were of the finest workmanship and materials; there was a sceptre of pink-veined marble with a gold-encased wooden handle. Behind one body lay four ceremonial axe-heads made of amber, lapis lazuli, obsidian, and nephrite, and the shaft holes were bound with gold and silver. The queen had been provided with her jewellery and a sceptre with a silver-encased handle. One tomb even contained fragments of a richly coloured carpet, the most ancient ever found. One of the sword blades was of iron, and there was a dagger with a silver blade engraved with little pictures of sailing ships, about the earliest known representations of ships outside Egypt. The household treasures of these Early Bronze Age rulers included vases, jugs, and bowls of gold and silver, and a particularly beautiful drinking vessel of fluted gold.

But perhaps the most remarkable and fortunate discovery, from an archaeological viewpoint, was part of what had been a gold-encased throne. On the fragments of gold leaf was the unmistakable cartouche of the Old Kingdom Egyptian pharaoh Sahure. The throne could have been a gift, but is more likely to have been acquired through trade. It enabled the discoverers to date the grave with some confidence to about 2500 B.C. This was about five hundred years before the Hittites moved westwards into Asia Minor.

An even richer find was made underneath the ruined Hittite

Stylized bronze stag from Alaja Huyuk.

city of Alaja Huyuk, in central Anatolia. Here, in 1935, a Turkish expedition penetrated to the deeper levels of the Hittite mound, hoping to find evidences of the pre-Hittite settlement. They found more than they had bargained for – a series of lavishly furnished tombs dating from the Early Bronze Age, about the same period as the Dorak graves. But these were much more elaborate. The method of burial recalls elements of both the Mycenaean shaft graves and the Scythian burials of a much later date. There were altogether thirteen interments, each consisting of a shaft cut into the burial mounds and covered by a roofing of logs, above which had been placed the skulls of sacrificed oxen.

As at Mycenae, the burials had not all been made at the same time. There was evidence that in at least one case a queen had preceded her husband by some years. When he died the grave was opened to admit his body. These tombs contained valuable offerings, including jewellery, toilet articles, ornaments, and weapons of high aesthetic quality. Many of them were of gold and silver, and displayed a technical quality hardly inferior to that of the Sumerian metalwork Woolley had discovered in the Ur death pits. On the other hand the vigorous animal portraiture, in the form of bronze bulls and stags, is faintly reminiscent of nomadic tribes of the Asian steppes. Other objects, of slightly later date, found at Horoztepe nearer the Black Sea, are even more strikingly similar to Scythian art than are the bronze animals.

At another site, Beycesultan, in western Anatolia, an archaeological expedition has recently unearthed the remains of a well-built city containing a palace with features recalling that of Knossos in Crete, although it is built mainly of mud brick, stone rubble, and timber. In a double shrine, probably dedicated to a male and female deity, worshippers had to make their offerings across a kind of altar shaped like the 'horns of consecration' in the Knossian palace. What used to be considered the characteristic Homeric or Mycenaean palace with its broad hall with central circular hearth and pillared porch – the megaron – also has been discovered at several places in Anatolia in an earlier context than that of Mycenae, Pylos, or Tiryns. These facts may point to an Anatolian origin of both the Minoan and Mycenaean peoples, though archaeologists differ on this matter.

Nevertheless one fact appears fairly clear. All these Bronze Age settlements were relatively small communities with a ruling aristocracy drawing its wealth and military manpower from a few score thousand peasants. Trade and cultural contacts there undoubtedly were, but on the whole each king ruled from his fortified city over a limited area. Maybe he entered into alliances with neighbouring princelings, married one of their daughters, and exchanged gifts and compliments, as did the Achaean nobility of the *Iliad*. There was as yet no unified state with a common social and economic system, as in

Babylonia and Egypt. The physical nature of Asia Minor, divided by mountain ranges, discouraged such a development and it required the energy and daring of the Hittites to bring about at least a temporary and partial unification.

The Hittites spoke an Indo-European language akin to Sanskrit, Greek, and most European tongues. They entered Anatolia early in the second millennium B.C., possibly in the same migratory movement that brought the Mycenaeans, or Achaeans, into Greece. Like the Mycenaeans, the ancestors of the Hittites found a Bronze Age people living in the land which they invaded. The Hittites acquired the name of the conquered territory – Hatti – in the same way that the Anglo-Saxon invaders of the British Isles took on the original name of the island Britain.

Conquest and unification were a very slow process. Hittite records found at Boghazkoy state that

> at first the land was small, but wherever he marched to battle he [Labarnas, an early king] subdued the lands of his enemies with might. He destroyed the lands and made them powerless, and he made the seas his frontiers.

The successor to Labarnas was Hattusilis I, in whose reign the Hittites began to move southwards, beyond the Taurus, into Syria, and to the south-east, no doubt attracted by the riches of the older civilizations long established in Mesopotamia. Hattusilis I had a warlike grandson, Mursilis I, who conquered Babylon in about 1600 B.C., just around the time the Seventeenth Dynasty pharaohs were liberating Egypt from the rule of the Hyksos.

During the fifteenth century B.C. the Hittites came into conflict with the Hurrians, who had occupied an area bordering the northern Euphrates. It was at this time that the great warrior Pharaoh Tuthmosis III was leading his conquering armies into northern Syria; it was he, and not the Hittite king, who eventually crushed the Hurrians and took the pressure off the Hittite frontier. Indeed, the Hittites may well have been valued allies of the Egyptians at this point, and if so, this would have been the first contact between the established imperial power of ancient Egypt and the newly emergent nation of the mountain-dwelling people.

When an Indo-European ruling caste known as the Mitanni later established sway over the Hurrians, they entered into friendly relations with the pharaohs Amenhotep III and Amenhotep IV (Akhenaten). Egypt was going through a non-militant phase and for a time the Mitanni were the most potent power in western Asia. Once again the Mitanni-ruled Hurrians gave great trouble to the Hittites, detaching their vassal states and threatening Hatti itself. The Hittites apparently suffered assault from various directions. One of their later chronicles, which seem to refer to this period, states that

> . . . the Hatti lands were sacked from beyond their borders. The enemy from Kaska came and sacked the Hatti lands and made Nenassa his frontier. From beyond the Lower Land came the enemy from Arzawa, and he too sacked the Hatti lands and made ... [a new] frontier.

Two Hittite kings of this period, Hattusilis II and Tudhaliyas III, struggled against the formidable power of the Mitanni, but with little success. It was one of Tudhaliyas' successors, the great Suppiluliumas, who turned the tide. Suppiluliumas might be called the Tuthmosis III of Hatti, a fighter, a cunning strategist, wise in the ways of war and diplomacy. However, it may have been fortunate for him that he did not have to meet the great Tuthmosis himself in battle. The Egypt to which he was opposed was peacefully concerned with its own affairs. The heretic Akhenaten was a pacifist and a dreamer, preoccupied with his religious reforms; he apparently disregarded the threats to his border lands.

After first suffering defeat at the hands of the Mitannian king, Tushratta, Suppiluliumas devised a new and daring plan. Crossing the Euphrates near Malatya, and traversing wild and dangerous country peopled by hostile tribes, he took the Mitanni in the rear. He recovered his lost provinces and sacked the Mitannian capital. Evidently shaken by this unexpected attack the king of Mittani avoided battle. Suppiluliumas had disposed of his ancient enemy. Once again the Hittite armies began to roll southwards and found themselves near the frontiers of Egyptian influence. It is possible that at this stage Suppiluliumas would have been content to establish his boundary on the Orontes, in Syria, and withdraw. But one of Egypt's vassals, the king of Kadesh, came out and offered battle. His armies were destroyed in the terrifying charge of the Hittite chariotry, and Suppiluliumas, carried forward by the impetus of his advance, pressed on into the Levant. The Hittites had come far from their mountain homeland, and from that rich coastal strip between the Lebanese mountains and the Great Green Sea, the Mediterranean, they turned their gaze south towards the gates of Egypt. The time of the Hittite advance was about 1370 B.C.

The rough highlanders from beyond the Taurus, with their chariots and horses and their powerful leader, encamped in Lebanon, while the petty kings of Syria, former vassals of Egypt, came to the tent of Suppiluliumas bearing tribute. And only a few hundred miles to the south lay the greatest power on earth, with a civilization stretching back more than fifteen hundred years to a time when the ancestors of the newly mighty Hittites may have been only skin-clad barbarians living in a primitive Stone Age society.

After another thirty years of arduous campaigning, during which he had battled with the Assyrians and consolidated his hold on Syria, the Hittite king, now an old man, was encamped near Carchemish, on the upper Euphrates. After an eight-day siege that great fortress surrendered, and the army was resting after its victory. Then a messenger arrived from Egypt, carrying a letter – one of the familiar baked-clay cuneiform tablets. When his secretary read the message to him the old king could not at first believe it, for it purported to be from the queen of Egypt.

> My husband has died [she wrote] and I have no son, but of you it is said that you have many sons. If you would send me one of your sons, he could become my husband. I will on no account take one of my subjects and make him my husband. I am very much afraid.

This letter was found by Winckler among the archives of Hattusas, the Hittite capital. Unfortunately there were no copies of the king's replies to this and further letters from the queen, which had evidently caused her some annoyance. He seems to have been sceptical about her overtures. Her next letter reads:

Why do you say, 'They are deceiving me'? If I had a son, would I write to a foreigner to publish my distress and that of my country? You have insulted me in speaking thus. . . . My husband is dead and I have no son. I will never take one of my subjects and marry him. I have written to no one but you. Everyone says you have many sons; give me one of them that he may become my husband.

Archaeology, which all too often has to concern itself with scraps of pottery, rarely stumbles on such a human story as this. The Egyptian queen who wrote those letters was almost certainly Ankheshamen, the girl-queen of Tutankhamen, widowed when the young pharaoh died at the age of about eighteen. According to Egyptian custom the next pharaoh could only legitimize his succession by marrying the royal heiress, in this case, Ankheshamen. Surrounded by intriguing, power-hungry courtiers and politicians, such as Ay, who had been Akhenaten's chief minister, the queen looked around desperately for an escape. Hence her statement, 'I will never take one of my subjects and marry him.' (Ay was already an elderly man, which may have had some bearing on the reasons underlying the girl's desperation.)

While her husband's youthful body soaked for the customary one hundred days in its natron bath, before embalmment and burial, she tried to bring off a coup that could defeat the intriguers who hoped to ride to power by marrying the pharaoh's heiress. She was probably not more than sixteen when she wrote those letters, and yet there is in them a feminine imperiousness worthy of Cleopatra. 'You have insulted me in speaking thus. . . . Everyone says you have many sons; give me one of them. . . .'

But Suppiluliumas, when he moved, moved too late. The end of the story is tragic. When one of the sons of the Hittite king was at last sent to Egypt, he never reached Thebes; possibly he was murdered by one of Ay's agents. And the Egyptian king-lists show that the next pharaoh was Ay – the man who is depicted on the wall of Tutankhamen's burial chamber, making due offerings to the *ka* of the dead pharaoh, had himself become a god-king.

When Suppiluliumas died the Hittite empire, which stretched from Anatolia to southern Syria, was the dominant power in western Asia, and the chief rival of Egypt. Eventually, of course, the two clashed. It was in 1300 B.C. at Kadesh, on the Orontes, that the great battle we have referred to earlier took place. Here the chariotry of Ramesses II met that of the Hittites; Egypt claimed success, but it was only Ramesses' bravery and energy that enabled the Egyptians to escape a crushing defeat. Yet, in the customary manner of the pharaohs – omnipotent as they traditionally made themselves appear – he caused to be carved those colossal temple reliefs of the battle that no visitor to Thebes can escape and that proclaimed his total victory. In fact, more wall space was devoted to this battle than to any other event in the history of Egypt. Later, however, Ramesses signed a mutual defence treaty with a subsequent Hittite king, Hattusilis III, copies of which were preserved both at Karnak and at Boghazkoy. As we have also already observed, Ramesses even married a Hittite princess and was delighted with his bride.

The adversaries of the Hittites were not confined to their southern neighbours in Syria and those at the borders of the land of Hatti. There were fresh disturbances in Asia Minor as well. Among the tablets found at Boghazkoy were some letters referring to a certain man named Attarissiyas who had evidently been troubling the Hittites; he had driven one of the Hittite king's vassals from his kingdom in western Anatolia. From this correspondence it appears that the Hittite king treated the king of Akaiwasha, over whom he had no jurisdiction, as an equal. There is a reference to a city in Asia Minor called, in Hittite, Millawanda, a city outside the control of the Hittite monarch but under the indirect control of the king of Akaiwasha. The correspondence also refers to a principality called Zippasla, which was given to the displaced vassal.

Letters like these give us many still-puzzling references to the political geography of western Anatolia; scholars compare words from Hittite texts with Greek words in an effort to learn whether the two great cultures were in contact. Now the name which Homer gave to the Mycenaean Greeks was the Achaeans, linguistically a word not unlike Akaiwasha, and we know that the name of the father of Agamemnon and Menelaus – the Atridae – was Atreus, which, it has been suggested, might be

Ramesses II's Hittite bride enters his presence.

compared with Attarissiyas. Millawanda was very likely the ancient Greek colony of Miletus, on the Aegean coast of Asia Minor, where a Mycenaean settlement has been unearthed. It is tempting to think that the kingdom of Akaiwasha was Mycenaean Greece itself; or was it a Mycenaean domain on the mainland of Anatolia, or, as has also been suggested by scholars, was it the island of Rhodes where the Achaean Greeks were established in considerable force? Are we stretching coincidence too far in seeking to compare a name recorded in a Hittite document with Greek names of lands and people of whom there is contemporary record? Here is another of those fascinating areas of speculation where, as has so often happened in the case of lost worlds rediscovered, archaeology and legend may prove to be in accord.

Still another cuneiform tablet records the fact that a king of Akaiwasha sent his sons to the court of the Hittite king in order to be trained in chariotry and horsemanship. We know from the *Iliad* that the chariot was the aristocratic arm of the Mycenaean Greek forces. Did they perhaps learn their craft from their neighbours in Asia Minor? The Hittites in turn, who were notable charioteers, probably took the idea of the chariot from the 'horse-rearing Mitanni' of the upper Euphrates, with whom they were in contact in the course of years both in peace and war.

Among the occasional adversaries of the Hittites were the kings of Arzawa, the land referred to in the tablets found at

A sword-eater swallows his sword as an acrobat balances on a free-standing ladder in this relief from Alaja Huyuk.

el Amarna and, obviously, no longer to be identified with the land of Hatti. In the latter part of the fourteenth century B.C. the Hittite king Mursilis II sent a challenge to the king of Arzawa that was in effect a declaration of war.

> My subjects who went over to you, when I demanded them back from you, you did not restore them to me. Up then! Let us fight, and let the storm god, my lord, decide our case!

Apparently the storm god favoured Mursilis and his cause, for the campaign records state that

> I, my Majesty, brought back to the royal palace [from Arzawa] 66,000 civilian captives; but what the lords, the soldiers, and the charioteers of Hattusas brought back in the way of civilian captives, oxen, and sheep – there was no counting it.

But unfortunately at this time, we are unable to ascertain just where Arzawa was.

Although records tell us much of the Hittites' military exploits they tell us little about the people and the manner in which they lived. From the pictures they have left of themselves they do not appear as a particularly attractive people; they

This relief, showing a lion hunt, comes from Malatya, a city which maintained Hittite tradition after Hattusas, the capital, fell.

were short, stocky, broad-shouldered mountain folk, hardy and active. Both men and women wore long woollen robes and stout upturned boots as a protection against the winter snows. Their principal cities somewhat resembled those of the Mycenaeans – citadels on easily defended hills, with strong walls and towers. The kings and nobles lived in relatively small palaces within the enclosing walls; other houses of merchants and farmers stood outside, but near the citadel. At Boghazkoy cattle and men were protected by an additional and more extensive outer wall.

The Hittites were certainly clever strategists, and, toughened by their life in the mountains, doughty fighters; but there is no evidence that their conquests were accompanied by the refined cruelties that the Assyrians inflicted on their defeated foes. A conquered city was given humane treatment; its people were spared, provided due tribute was paid. If the city resisted it was looted, burned, and its inhabitants made slaves; but they were apparently not mutilated or tortured. They appear to have had a rough but genuine humanity which is reflected in some of their laws that have been found. Many of

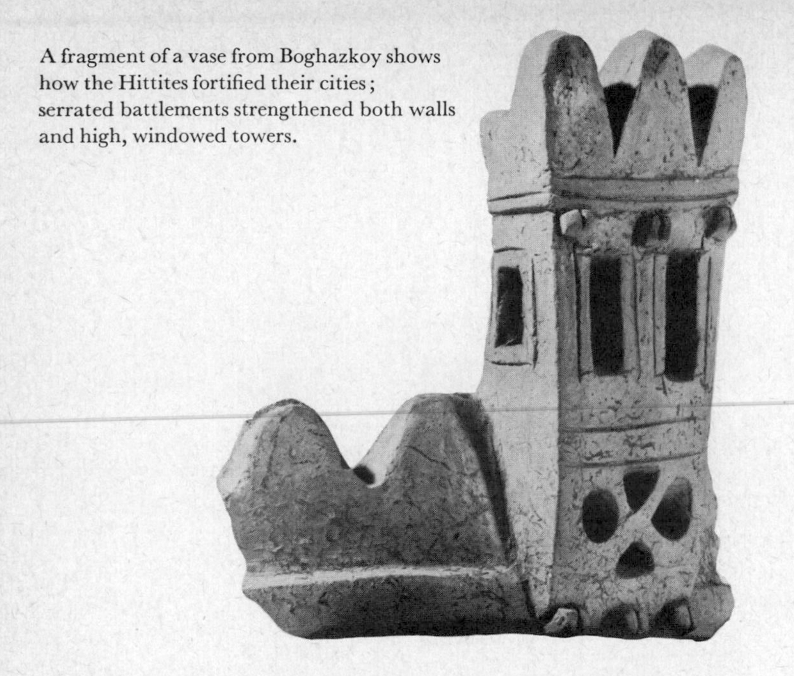

A fragment of a vase from Boghazkoy shows how the Hittites fortified their cities; serrated battlements strengthened both walls and high, windowed towers.

these are essentially the practical, down-to-earth laws of a peasant people. For instance:

> If a pig goes upon a threshing floor or a field or a garden, and the owner of the meadow, the field, or the garden smites it so that it die, he shall give it back to its owner; but if he does not give it back he becomes a thief. . . . If anyone borrows and yokes an ox, a horse, a mule, or an ass and it dies, or a wolf devours it, or it goes astray, he shall pay in full value; but if he say 'by the hand of a god it died', then he shall take the oath.

However, as in all ancient civilizations there was a clear distinction between freeman and slave, with varying conditions for the treatment of each class. The Hittite king tells his garrison commanders:

> Into whatever city you return, summon forth all the people of the city. Whoever has a suit, decide it for him and satisfy him. If the slave of a man, or the maidservant of a man has a suit, decide it for them and satisfy them. Do not make the better case the worse or the worse case the better. *Do what is just.*

A strangely shaped stamp, possibly showing gods and cult scenes.

As in Egypt, there were in Anatolia a large number of local and regional religious cults; and as in Egypt these continued to exist long after the Hittite state was unified and a state religion had developed. The king was the high priest of this cult, and there exist many cuneiform tablets that give us the names and functions of the gods, and the prayers addressed to them by the royal family. There are also a number of myths and poems of religious character, but it is strange that these do not appear to refer to the principal deities of the state religion. It has been suggested that this religious literature was derived from the local cults.

In many parts of central Anatolia there are rock-cut sculptures, possibly depicting these deities. The most impressive are those at Yazilikaya (the Turkish word meaning *inscribed rock*), near Boghazkoy, which Winckler visited early in this century. Here, in a narrow cleft in the rock, gods and goddesses march in two processions towards a central point, each carrying a symbol that can be recognized although with difficulty. These sculptured reliefs reveal the curious fact that, by the thirteenth century B.C., the Hittites had apparently based their state religion on deities adopted from their once formidable enemies, the Hurrians. Among these deities some can be identified with certainty, despite the weathering of the rock over a period of some three thousand years; they include Ea, god of the Nether Sea, who originated in Sumer; Shaushka, goddess of love and fertility, derived from the Mesopotamian Ishtar; Halki, god of grain; Kushukh, the moon god; the sun god, whose name is unknown; and Hesui, who was an underworld deity.

But the most important deity to the Hittites was the weather god Teshub, who occupied a central position at Yazilikaya. His consort Hebat (or Hepit) was almost as important as he was. Teshub has some similarity to Olympian Zeus; he is often shown standing alone, grasping a symbolic bolt of lightning in one hand and an axe in the other. His sacred animal was the bull, on which he is sometimes shown standing. It is natural that the Hittites, who lived in a land subject to frequent, violent storms, should have given precedence to a god who manifested himself in thunder and lightning, as it was natural to the ancient Egyptians, living under cloudless skies, to honour Re above all other deities. On the other hand, some state deities have their equivalents in ancient religions of different lands; the fertility goddess for example can be equated with the Egyptian Hathor, the Babylonian Ishtar, and the Greek Aphrodite. There was also Telipinu, a god of agriculture and son of Teshub. One of the hymns represents the weather god as saying, 'This son of mine is mighty; he harrows and ploughs, he irrigates the fields and makes the crops grow.'

Despite the establishment of the state cult at Hattusas, one gets the impression that in Hatti the independent spirit of the people frustrated any attempt that may have been made by the systematizing theologians of Hattusas to bring the whole realm under one tidy religious system. For instance, although Teshub the weather god was supreme at Hattusas itself, at

'King of Heaven, Lord of Hatti', the weather god Teshub officially shared the divine throne with the sun goddess, who 'directed the government of Hatti' from Arinna, a local cult centre.

Arinna, a cult centre some distance from the capital, he was merely the consort of a sun goddess, Wurusemu. Could it be that in Anatolia, as in pre-Hellenic Greece, there was conflict between an earlier religion, dominated by female deities, and a later cult in which male gods were predominant?

There is possibly an intriguing example of this in the presence of two sun deities, a god and a goddess. The Hittite king Muwatallis addresses this prayer to the sun god:

> Sun god of heaven, my lord, shepherd of mankind! Thou risest, O sun god of heaven, from the sea and goest up to heaven. O sun god of heaven, my lord, daily thou sittest in judgement upon man, dog, pig, and wild beasts of the field.

Yet the sun goddess is described as

> Queen of the Land of Hatti, Queen of Heaven and Earth, Mistress of the kings and queens of the Land of Hatti, directing the government of the Land of Hatti.

And the husband of Wurusemu was not the sun god but the weather god Teshub.

Because of these varying godly alliances, it is difficult to gain an altogether clear picture of Hittite religion. Their state chronicles, on the other hand, were written with clarity and directness; reading the recorded statements of some of the Hittite kings is almost like listening to a verbatim report. One king, Hattusilis I, had named his nephew Labarnas as his successor, but the young prince had caused trouble. So the king assembled his fighting men and dignitaries and said to them:

> Behold, I have fallen sick. The young Labarnas I had proclaimed to you, saying, 'He shall sit upon the throne.' I, the king, called him my son, embraced him, exalted him, cared for him continually. But he showed himself a youth not fit to be seen; he shed no tears, he showed no pity; he was cold and heartless. I, the king, summoned him to my couch and said, 'Well! No one will in future bring up the child of his sister as a foster son! The word of the king he has not laid to his heart, but the word of his mother, that serpent, he has laid to his heart. . . . Enough! He is my son no more!'

Then, the chronicle goes on,

> His mother bellowed like an ox: 'They have torn asunder the womb in my living body! They have ruined him, and you will kill him!' 'But have I, the king, done him any evil? ... Behold I have given my son Labarnas a house; I have given him arable land in plenty; sheep in plenty I have now given him. ... Behold Mursilis is now my son. In place of the lion the god will set up another lion. And in the hour when the call to arms goes forth, you, my servants and leading citizens, must be at hand to help my son. ...'

It is straightforward and imposing, with a ring of personality that is lacking in the more formal records of the Egyptian and Mesopotamian rulers.

An equally vivid record describes the anger of a king when, at the siege of an enemy town, 'they broke the battering ram. The king waxed wroth', the chronicle continues, 'and his face was grim; "They constantly bring me evil tidings!".' Then he blistered his inefficient officers with the words, 'May the weather god carry you away in a flood! Be not idle! Make a battering ram in the Hurrian manner and let it be set in its place!'

Although the Hittites appear to have borrowed much of their art, their culture, their religion, and – importantly – a convenient writing system from their more highly developed Mesopotamian neighbours, they come to life in their own right in their surviving documents, as in the furious exhortation of the king just quoted. They were a rugged, independent people – energetic, determined, probably coarse and rough, a people toughened by hardship and adversity, adventurous and brave, not afraid to march down from their mountain strongholds and challenge the older, more sophisticated peoples of Mesopotamia and Egypt.

They lived by agriculture, stock-raising, and trade, exchanging their copper, silver, and iron (Anatolia was rich in minerals) for the textiles and other goods produced in Syria and Mesopotamia. The smelting of iron in commercial quantities was to revolutionize the ancient world, and this technique is believed to have originated in Asia Minor. The metal had been known long before, but it was not until an unidentified

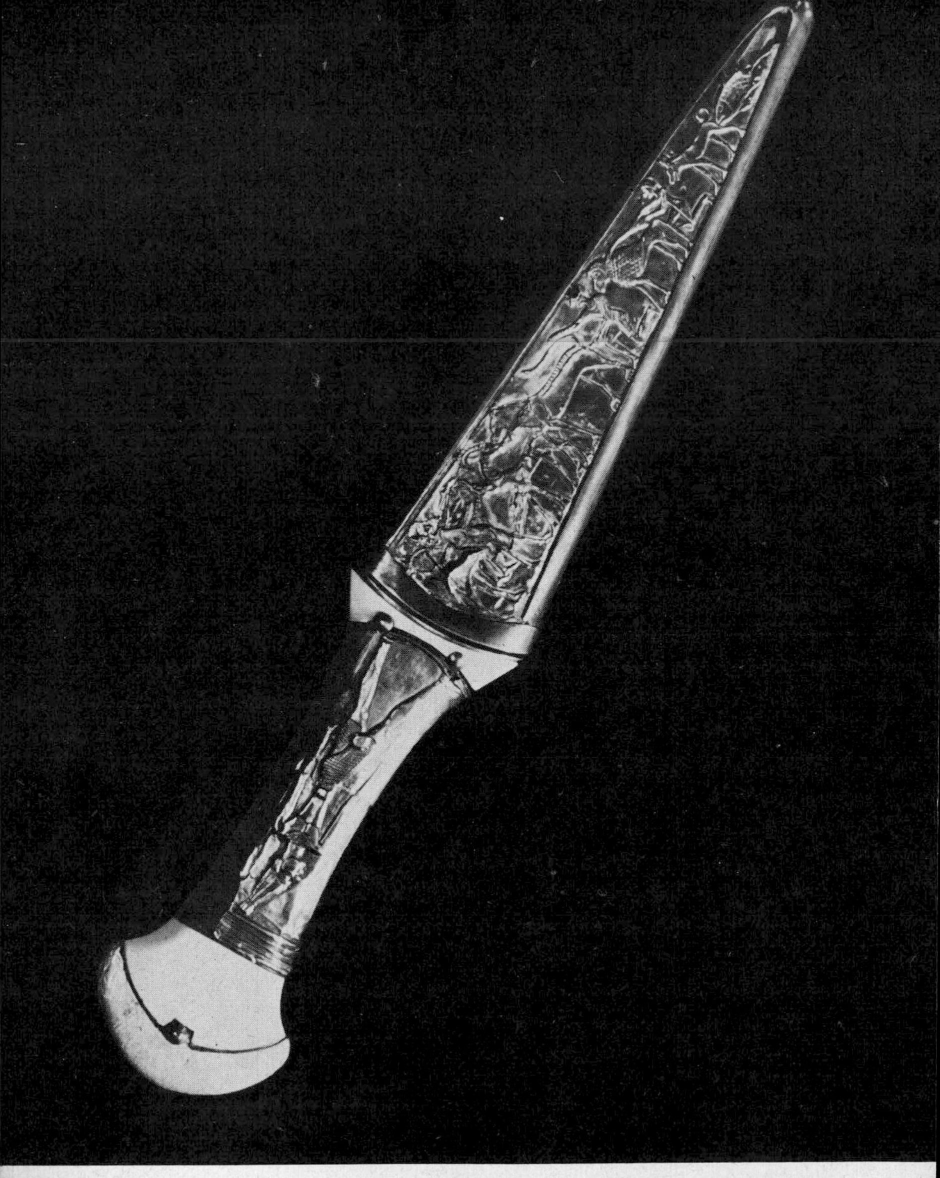

From a Byblos temple of the second millennium, the gold scabbard shows a mixture of Syrian and Egyptian motifs whereas the metalworking

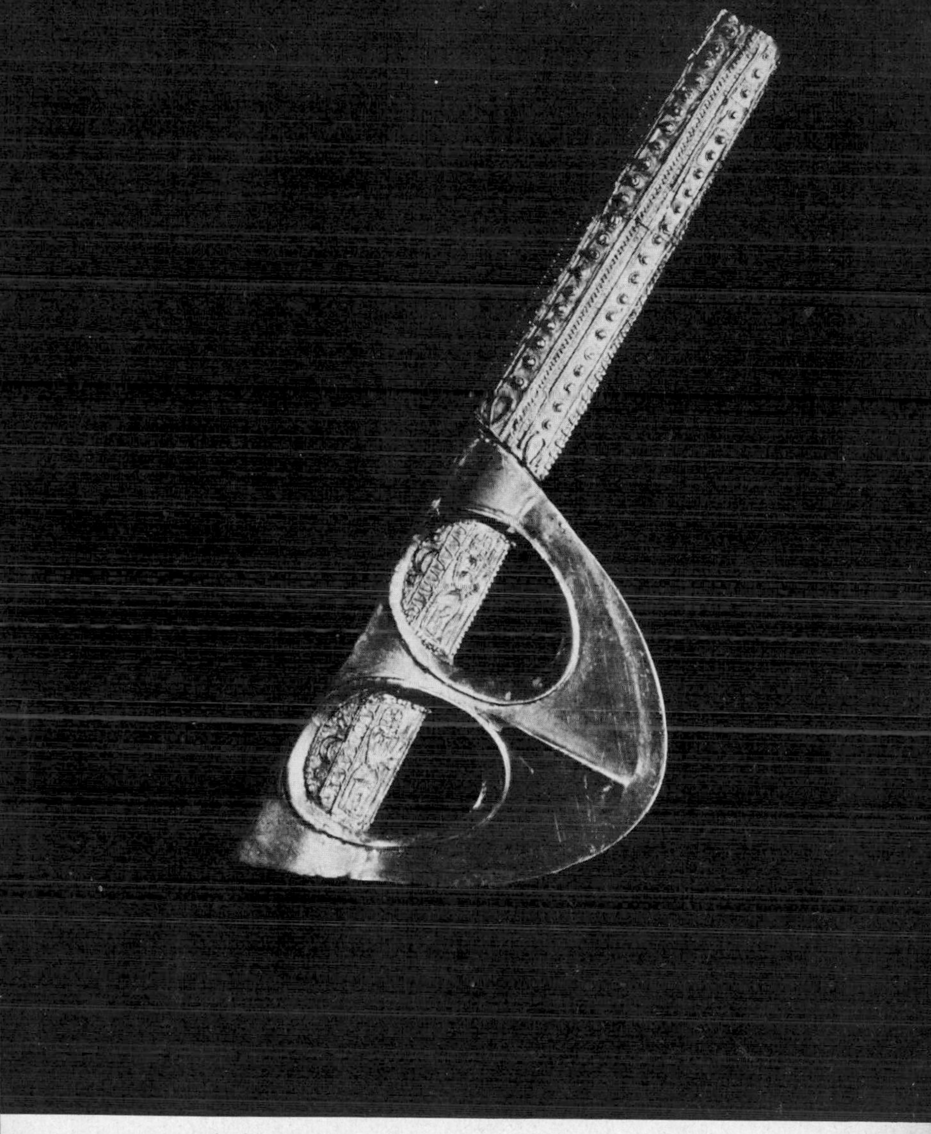

methods, seen also on the crescent-bladed axe, are typically Amorite and Syrian.

people (perhaps the Chalybees in the Armenian mountains) discovered the secret of making it cheaply that it spread across the world.

Another letter from a Hittite king to a fellow monarch is worth quoting in this connexion:

As for the good iron which you wrote about to me, good iron is not available in my seal-house [a storage place for worked iron] in Kizzuwatna. That it is a bad time for producing iron I have written. They will produce good iron, but as yet they will not have finished. When they have finished I shall send it to you. Today now I am dispatching an iron dagger blade to you.

When this letter was written, in the thirteenth century B.C., the Iron Age had not begun. The noblemen of Egypt, Babylon, and Mycenae were still using bronze weapons. In the tomb of Tutankhamen (fourteenth century B.C.) was found one of the pharaoh's most valuable possessions – a ceremonial dagger with a hilt of gold and semi-precious stones, but a blade of iron, more precious than the gold and jewels. The rest of the king's weapons were merely of bronze.

Although there were obviously iron deposits in their territory and although equally obviously they were familiar with the metal, the Hittites remained essentially a Bronze Age people. With the more general use of iron for tools and weapons the face of ancient society was changed beyond recognition. It was in the dawn of the Iron Age that the inhabitants of Asia Minor were thrown into complete confusion by waves of invading peoples who appear at the beginning of the twelfth century B.C. This was, as we have seen in earlier chapters, a time of international disturbance and unrest.

In Anatolia itself one displaced tribe cannoned into the next, displacing it in turn, like billiard balls. The Hittites were swept down from the mountains into the hills and valleys of northern Syria. These lands were not totally unfamiliar to them for some of their culture had been implanted south of the Taurus during the centuries their imperial legions had battled with the Mitanni, the Assyrians, and local princelings on the Syrian plains. Long before the fall of Hattusas, the populations of many of these cities included Hittite elements, along with Aramean and Hurrian, and it was perhaps then that the builders of

A fragment of an ivory box lid from the port of Ras Shamra shows a goddess who is part Aegean and part Asian.

Carchemish and Malatya, among others, had begun to borrow from Anatolian traditions. The style that resulted was a blend, however, difficult to date or to separate into its various components, and although Hittites surely settled in this north Syrian region, the only record of them we have during this murky period of history is the occasional Assyrian reference to the area as 'the land of Hatti'. There seems to have been enough recognizably Hittite influence – along with their hieroglyphs – to lead some experts to call these cities, unearthed by archaeologists some fifty years ago, Neo- or Syro-Hittite.

Portrayed on a terracotta panel, a Phrygian soldier marches to war.

There is much that is still obscure, but it has been suggested that this may offer an explanation of the biblical Hittites at a period long after the Anatolian Hittites had been dispersed. The rulers and inhabitants of such north Syrian towns may not even have been of Hittite stock, but rather peoples who had absorbed various elements of the culture of the Hittites.

We have lingered over the Hittites and their empire because of all the heterogeneous peoples who occupied Asia Minor in ancient times, their story is most fully documented; and because it was the search for the Hittites that turned the attention of archaeologists to the hitherto little-known Anatolia. Here, at what had been the centre of Hittite power, a different people emerged during the centuries following 1200 B.C. – the Phrygians, a people of the Iron Age.

Apart from giving their name to the conical hat which became a symbol of revolution in eighteenth-century France, the Phrygians have best been remembered chiefly for their king, Midas of the golden touch, whose legendary avarice was used by the Greeks to adorn a moral tale. But there may have been a King Midas – probably several bearing the same name. The word *Mitas* occurs in Assyrian records, and at Gordium, the Phrygian capital where Alexander cut the Gordian knot, the University of Pennsylvania made a sensational discovery as recently as 1957. At the site, which stands near the Sangarius River, there is an artificial hill about one hundred feet high, known by tradition as the Tomb of Midas. The American archaeologists, who had already done some notable and valuable work in excavating the city, decided to investigate the tomb, using modern methods. Instead of laboriously trenching into the hill, they drilled a small hole in the top and eventually came upon the roof of what appeared to be the tomb chamber. Then, starting again at ground level, they drove a tunnel horizontally through the earth until they came upon the stone retaining walls of the rubble mound which covered the wooden tomb chamber.

And then they struck trouble. Having breached this wall, they were forced to remove the greater part of the rubble filling in order to get at the chamber, so that eventually all that was left was an empty space under a heavy earthen covering, now deprived of most of its support. It required some courage to enter, but upon doing so at the risk of being buried alive, the Pennsylvania team was rewarded by an extraordinary sight. Near the middle of the chamber, on a bed that had

The Tarkondemos seal, on which a king appears; the ten cuneiform and six hieroglyphic signs constitute the first Hittite bilingual text found.

collapsed, lay the untouched body of a Phrygian king. In the glare of the floodlights they saw the skeleton, lying under the remains of some twenty coverlets. Against the wall rested rich furniture adorned and inlaid with rare woods. Scores of fine copper vessels had collapsed on to the floor. The cascade of metal, we are told, almost filled the chamber, shining in the brilliant green of oxidized copper. There were massive cauldrons for food, with their supporting tripods, and other articles that had laid with their owner for at least twenty-seven hundred years. But no gold – not a scrap or particle.

That might seem to dispose of the Midas legend – except, of course, there is no proof that this was Midas' sepulchre, assuming that the legendary king was a real person and not a myth. There certainly was an important Phrygian king named Midas who, according to Greek tradition, died during the Cimmerian invasion of about 680 B.C.

Our knowledge of both Phrygian and Hittite history is far from complete. One of the most puzzling problems was not solved until 1945, when archaeologists found the key to Hittite hieroglyphs – the mysterious writing noted by Burckhardt at Hamath that first put archaeologists on the trail of the Hittites. During and after the First World War the task of decipherment was left mainly to British and American scholars, while the Germans concentrated on the cuneiform version of the Hittite language. For many years there had been scant success since no bilingual clue appeared to exist. Then, in a remote, little-visited region of south-eastern Anatolia, the ancient Cilicia, a local schoolmaster reported that about five hours horse-ride from the town of Kadirili lay the site of a lost city.

In the autumn of 1945 the eminent German archaeologist H. T. Bossert, and his team, made their way there, to what had been the fortress city of Karatepe. Half hidden among the brambles, they found a battered, sculptured, half-human figure, lying face down, some sculptured lions with a standing human figure and, on the crown of the hill, extensive remains of walls with strong defensive gateways. Within one of these gateways the astonished archaeologists saw a series of crude sculptured scenes – a sea battle, an orchestra, a king feasting, and various sporting and religious activities. The art was obviously very late – much later than the period of the Hittite empire – but nevertheless the Hittite hieroglyphs were there carved on one side of the gateway. And, on the other side there were inscriptions in the known alphabetic script of Phoenicia; it was soon established that the two inscriptions, each in a different language, gave an identical message. The long-sought-for bilingual had been found at last.

Even so, the Hittite hieroglyphic script has still not been completely deciphered, though now it is only a matter of time and study. Much progress has already been made by the French scholar Emmanuel Laroche, and new discoveries of Hittite hieroglyphic seals at Ras Shamra in Syria have also helped to advance these investigations.

Obviously this story cannot hope to be complete. Today discoveries are being made in Asia Minor that will throw a keener light on what has been written and, no doubt, will call for revisions of current records. We are still only at the very beginning of the problem. But Anatolia, that hitherto neglected land of rich interest, is coming into its own at last.

4 The Enigmatic Etruscans

The world of Etruria is, in some ways, more mysterious and inaccessible than that of Egypt, Mesopotamia, Crete, or Mycenae, despite the fact that it is closer to us in time than any of these others. Unfortunately, the Etruscans cannot speak to us directly through their literature. Livy was told that a few generations before his time young Romans studied the Etruscan literature as conscientiously as they later did the Greek, but except for brief inscriptions, none of this has survived. The inscriptions are in letters much like the Greek, and can be read and pronounced, but they are only imperfectly understood. No Michael Ventris has yet come forward to decipher the Etruscan language.

In the later centuries of their development the Etruscans were well known to the Greeks and the Romans, both of whom fought them and wrote about them. Partly because of this ancient hostility the information provided by Greek and

A terracotta portrait, from the roof of an Etruscan temple at Veii, of the god Turms, who conducted the souls of the dead to the underworld; he was identical with the Greek Hermes.

Roman historians and commentators is often inaccurate and distorted. The Romans were the worse culprits, since they learned a great deal from the Etruscans, then virtually obliterated them as a separate entity, and finally slandered and vilified their memory. For impartial evidence we have to rely on the archaeological investigations of their cities and cemeteries, which are numerous, although they suffered almost two centuries of indiscriminate plundering before modern methods and skills were applied to excavation.

Ancient Etruria lay on the western side of Italy, between the Apennines and the Tyrrhenian Sea. It extended from the land about the Arno River in the north to the Tiber River in the south, and included modern Tuscany, which takes its name from the Etruscans. But at one period the Etruscans controlled Campania and the basin of the Po River, and had reached the northern Adriatic. Many of the most famous cities in Italy were originally Etruscan – Pisa, Arezzo, Cortona, Siena, Volterra, Orvieto, Perugia, Assisi, and others. (Rome itself was once an Etruscan centre; and the islands of Elba and Corsica were also Etruscan.) But there were other towns which were either deserted or which lost their former importance with the decline of Etruscan culture and it is mainly at these, such as Veii, Tarquinia, Cerveteri, and Chiusi (the ancient forms of these names were, respectively, Tarquinii, Caere, and Clusium), that archaeologists have found rich remains.

The Etruscan country varies between fertile plains, such as those near the Campanian coast and in Tuscany below Arezzo, and steep narrow valleys which cleave the Apennines. There are only two rivers of any size, the Arno and the Tiber, and these are navigable for but short stretches. The rest are mainly *torrenti* – dry boulder-strewn gullies in summer, roaring sluices of foam in winter. Vines, olives, and wheat grow in the lowlands; cattle graze on the lower hills, and goats and sheep on the higher slopes.

Tuscany is one of the most beautiful regions in Italy, and even those who have never seen it have admired it in the works of the great Florentine painters. It is therefore difficult to imagine Etruria as a rude and desolate country. Yet just over a century ago, even though the history of the Etruscans

Etruscan Italy.

had long been a subject of considerable investigation and speculation, the English traveller George Dennis could write of

remains of an ancient art completely unknown to the rest of the world, an object of the ignorant astonishment of peasants and ... still neglected; in a countryside almost decimated by malaria, never crossed by the educated and intelligent traveller, the most striking monuments may rest for centuries without attracting attention. ... I am convinced that Italy has been only half explored. ... In addition, ruins and remains are such common sights in this country that they excite no particular attention.

Where was this 'ancient art' that so excited Dennis and later explorers? Mainly in tomb-sites, which were often whole underground streets of sepulchres cut out of the rock and clearly designed to look like the earthly homes of their occupants. Sometimes the burials were found by accident – a peasant ploughing suddenly saw one of his draft oxen disappear into a hole in the ground, and there was a tomb – but more often they were dug for, or rather mined, by plunderers in search of saleable loot, or by amateur archaeologists searching for art objects with which to enrich their collections. Even as early as the eighteenth century a wave of 'Etruscomania' had swept across Europe; societies were formed for study; scholars examined ancient records and tried to decipher the Etruscan inscriptions; and the interest hardly abated over the years to come.

In time such an abundance of these treasures came to light that during the latter half of the nineteenth century, museums and private galleries overflowed with them – statues in stone, terracotta, and bronze; painted and figured pottery and gold vessels; domestic equipment such as lamps, candelabra, and engraved mirrors; and bracelets, fibulae, rings, and pendants. Some of these objects bore a resemblance to Roman forms, and many were created with a suavity and sensuousness that showed Greek influence; but they were neither Roman nor Greek. They were oriental in feeling, but they were clearly not oriental in origin. These remarkable finds, emerging into the sunlight of Italy after lying in darkness for more than twenty-four hundred years, had belonged to the mysterious Etruscans of whom the Greeks and Romans had written. Yet in spite of this abundant evidence and the research it stimulated, the Etruscans continue to remain an enigmatic people even to modern scholars.

We are not yet sure where they came from. Nearly all the ancient historians believed that they originated in Lydia, in Asia Minor, but most of these writers probably followed Herodotus. In the fifth century B.C. this Greek traveller described how a great famine had occurred in Lydia, and how after enduring this for many years, the Lydian king divided his people into two groups and cast lots to decide which group was to stay:

> He appointed ... his son Tyrrhenus to command the emigrants [who] ... went down to the coast at Smyrna, where they built vessels, put aboard all their household effects, and sailed in search of a livelihood elsewhere. They passed many countries and finally reached Umbria in the north of Italy, where they settled and still live to this day. Here they changed their name from Lydians to Tyrrhenians, after the king's son Tyrrhenus, who was their leader.

Herodotus has been proved right in so many instances that one hesitates to dismiss this story as a legend. Yet from the time of Dionysius of Halicarnassus, who lived in the first century A.D. and who questioned Herodotus' explanation, scholars have been divided between those who believe the Etruscans were the descendants of an Oriental people who modelled western Italy some time after 1000 B.C., and those who claim they were an indigenous race whose culture developed on Italian soil, but who were subject to influences from the east. The dispute still goes on.

One fact, however, is certain. At the beginning of the first millennium B.C. there was nothing in Italy, or in western Europe for that matter, worthy of the name of civilization. A primitive Bronze Age culture had existed for hundreds of years on the Italian peninsula, but nothing at all comparable to what had developed in the Aegean area. Then, about 1000 B.C., a wave of invaders – people who were familiar with the use of iron – entered Italy from the north, overcame the indigenes, and established themselves in what is now Tuscany, and other places both to the north and to the south on the peninsula.

This culture, called Villanovan from the type-site at Villanova (a suburb of Bologna), flourished most vigorously in the area about Tarquinia, Cerveteri, and Veii, which later was the heart of Etruscan civilization. With this new development, which is characterized by cremation burial, great importance was attached to the welfare of the dead. The cinerary urns, some of which are hut-shaped, probably in imitation of Villanovan dwellings, were buried in pits and surrounded by objects intended for the afterlife; men had their bronze and

Cinerary urn.

iron weapons, women their bronze fibulae, bronze and amber jewels, and combs, needles, and spindles. These are interesting, but in no way rich or elaborate; on stylistic grounds they can be dated between 1000 and 750 B.C.

This period corresponds to the so-called Dark Age in Greece, between the collapse of the brilliant civilizations of Crete and Mycenae and the dawn of the classical period. After two thousand years of high achievement Egypt had begun its slow decline. But powerful new civilizations were emerging. Assyria had begun its second rise to power, which reached a peak about 750 B.C. In Asia Minor the Phrygians had established themselves in the central plateau and the Lydians had become dominant in the south-west. The peoples of the Aegean and the Mediterranean world were in a ferment. Fresh waves of invaders poured down into southern Europe. The Phoenicians of the Levant, themselves under pressure from the east, had begun to move westward, establishing their great colony at Carthage on the North African coast and even getting a foothold in Spain. During this period the Dorian Greeks were also on the move, thrusting westwards in search of new lands and trading possibilities.

Towards the end of this period, some time in the eighth century B.C., there were dramatic changes in the Villanovan culture, changes that anticipate the splendid development of Etruscan civilization in the centuries that followed. The dead

Etruscan mausoleum. Household utensils have been modelled in stucco on the walls.

are no longer cremated; rather they are interred, first in ditch graves and later in stone-built, vaulted mausoleums covered with mounds of earth. The grave goods become richer, and different in character. There is a greater abundance of bronze objects, such as vases, helmets, and shields, which, although not the same as those used in the Aegean area, nevertheless resemble them.

The migrant Greeks could have been the intermediaries through which this eastern influence first appeared among the Villanovans. However, many of the innovations that appeared were certainly not Greek in origin. For instance, it seems hardly likely that, as has been claimed, there was any direct connexion between the domed mausoleums of seventh-century Etruria and the famous tholos tombs of Mycenae. In Greece the construction of such domed tumuli had been discontinued

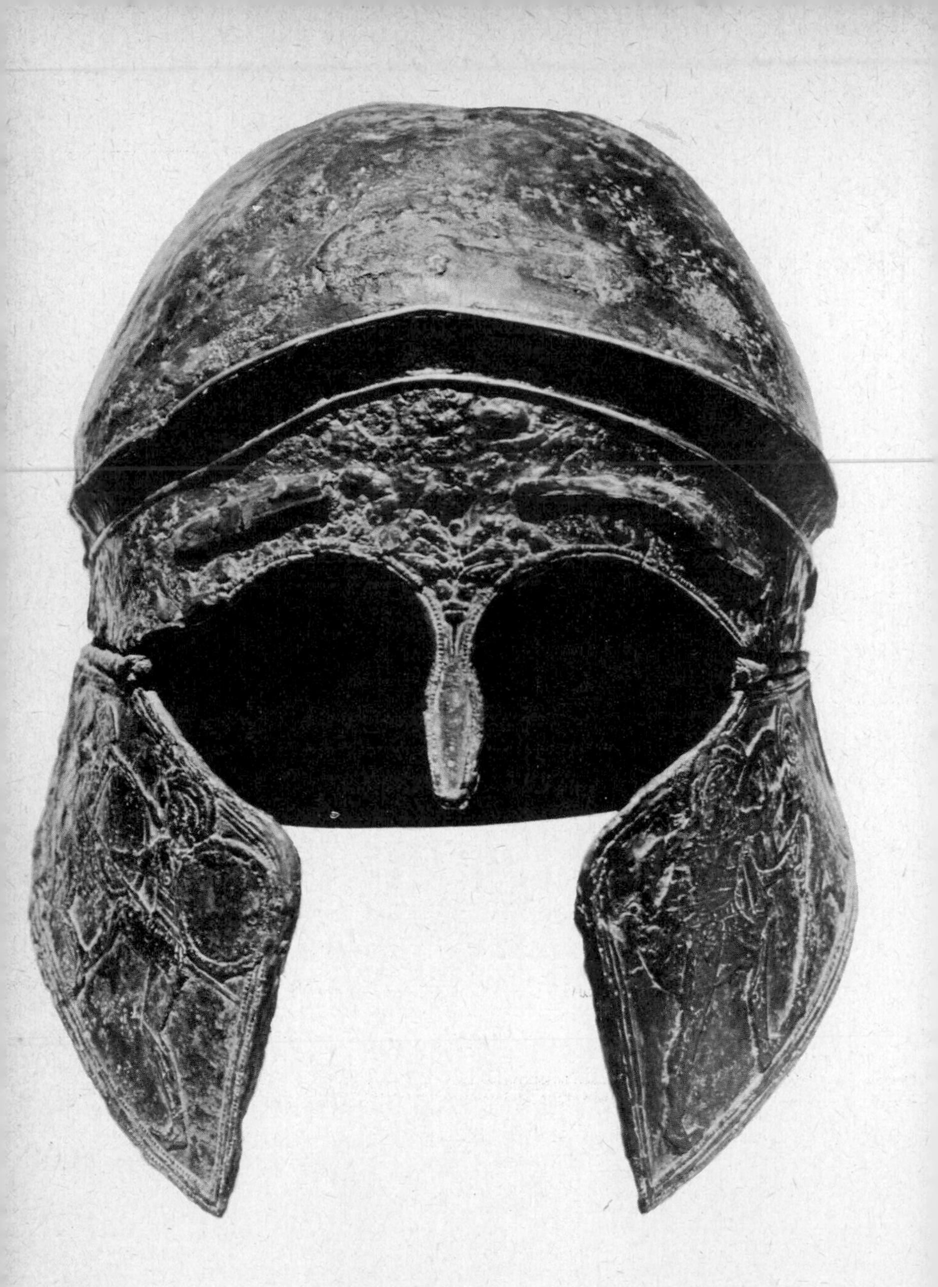

Ceremonial helmet, modelled after a Grecian prototype. The surface of both cheek-pieces is finely embossed with scenes of battle.

A terracotta sarcophagus found at Cerveteri shows an Etruscan aristocrat and his wife reclining together on a couch as if attending a banquet in the life hereafter.

centuries earlier, in the late Bronze Age. In Asia Minor, on the other hand, they were being built well into the Iron Age, as witnessed by the famous Tomb of Midas at Gordium. If there was a connexion between developments in Etruria and regions to the east it is more likely to have been with Anatolia than with Greece.

This Oriental connexion, so long ago suggested by Herodotus, is indicated, though not proved by any means, by numerous other parallels. To name a few: as in the case of many eastern peoples, Etruscan religion was a revealed religion; a god or spirit named Tages had in the remote past dictated its principles, and these immutable laws had been written down and transmitted by the priests to succeeding generations. It was a highly ritualistic religion, and it made great use of divination by signs. Such a conception was common in the ancient east, but not among the Indo-European peoples of the west. The Etruscan name for themselves, Rasenna, is found in various forms in Asia Minor. On the island of Lemnos, in the Aegean, archaeologists discovered inscriptions in a language which is

remarkably like ancient Etruscan. If the Etruscans came from Anatolia it would be natural for some of them to have occupied Lemnos, which is a few miles off the coast. As further evidence, in tomb paintings depicting the earthly life of the Etruscans, women are given an honoured place. We see them banqueting with male guests and being embraced by their husbands. Sometimes the names of the female as well as the male ancestors of the deceased are mentioned in funerary inscriptions. Such was not the attitude of the Greeks towards their womenfolk, though it was a characteristic of some of the older Oriental civilizations.

It seems likely that Greek influences had little to do with the earliest development of the Etruscan nation. But the story is different later. When the Etruscans finally were exposed to Greek culture, they enthusiastically adapted it to their own. Indeed one scholar has recently suggested that '... getting to know Homer was one of the most important experiences of

Part lion, part serpent and part goat, the chimera [opposite] was derived from Greek mythology, like the gorgon here.

the dawning Etruscan civilization . . .'. The aristocrats of Etruria modelled themselves on the heroes of Mycenae, and the major Etruscan gods were closely identified with the divinities of Greece. Etruscan artists found it appropriate to decorate tombs and vases with scenes from Greek mythology, scenes which were apparently readily understood by the public, and as early as the seventh century B.C., there were Greek vase painters working in Cerveteri. The Etruscan alphabet itself is of Greek origin, probably derived from a variant of the standard Greek alphabet used by Hellenic colonists in the town of Cumae, near Naples. In the commercial centres, such as Cumae, Greek and Etruscan merchants settled alongside each other.

Setting aside all questions of the still debatable racial origins of the Etruscans, it is a matter of overriding importance that their culture took on its distinctive form at a time when the Greeks and other migrants from the east were founding settlements and pushing their trading ventures into the western

Mediterranean area. The west had much to offer these newcomers. Its lands were for the most part sparsely populated and occupied by relatively primitive peoples who were incapable of developing their own resources. There were copper and iron in Italy and elsewhere, silver in Spain, and tin in far-off Cornwall in the British Isles, to which the Phoenicians gained access.

In this struggle for raw materials, in which Greeks contested with Phoenicians, Etruria stood in a key position. The main source of Etruria's wealth and prosperity was her mineral deposits, of which other Mediterranean powers were envious. In the northern part of Etruria were the hills known today as the Colline Metallifere (Metalliferous Hills), rich in iron, zinc, tin, and copper. The gold, silver, ivory, and other precious materials that the Etruscans later imported to adorn their bodies, their homes, and eventually their tombs can only have been obtained in exchange for these valuable minerals. The Greeks who had already founded trading colonies along the western coast of Italy, at Paestum, Cumae, Naples, and elsewhere before 600 B.C., were well aware of these riches. They had also established themselves in Sicily, southern Gaul (at Marseille), North Africa, and even Spain, where they had little difficulty in exploiting the natural resources of the hinterland. But in Italy they confronted an intelligent, well-organized, civilized people, both appreciative of the natural riches of the land they occupied and capable of capitalizing on them.

Etruria had resources other than metals. It had dense forests which both provided timber and sheltered abundant game; the climate was kindly, the plains fertile, and the foothills offered abundant pasturage. There were good harbours, and a long sea coast from which mariners could set out on adventurous journeys to other lands.

That the Etruscans were skilful and formidable sailors we know from the Greeks. One of their legends tells how Etruscan mariners even succeeded in capturing the Greek god Dionysus, who only escaped by changing his captors into dolphins. In these Greek stories the Etruscans appear to be ruthless pirates, as no doubt they often were. On one occasion they descended

Wearing the broad-brimmed hat characteristic of his class, an Etruscan peasant walks behind his team of yoked oxen. A votive offering, this model is one of the few Etruscan bronzes that represent a scene of rural life.

on the sanctuary of Artemis at Brauron, near Athens, possibly because it not only possessed rich treasures but was served by young priestesses. Incidents such as these did not make the Greeks love the Etruscans (and help to explain an anti-Etruscan bias in later Greek writings), but they prove what a power these pre-Roman rulers of western Italy must have been. Greece, wrote Dionysius of Halicarnassus, was 'full of the name of Etruria'.

Since we are concerned here with the world of the Etruscans rather than with their political history, the latter need only be briefly sketched. During the period 700 to 500 B.C., the Etruscan coastal cities, such as Cerveteri, Tarquinia, and Vetulonia, sent out fleets which sailed venturously along the coasts of Provence, Spain, and North Africa, mixing legitimate trading with profitable piracy. In so doing they encountered their chief rivals, the Greeks and the Carthaginians, whom they often fought with zest and success. For a short time Etruria dominated the western seas as the Mycenaeans had earlier dominated the Aegean.

But when the Greek colonists, having already established themselves in Sicily and southern Italy, began settling in Corsica, the Etruscans allied themselves with Carthage against the Hellenes. After a major naval battle in 540 B.C. the Greeks evacuated Corsica, but though the Etruscans had removed one danger, Carthage profited most from the victory. From then on she dominated the western Mediterranean and guarded the Straits of Gibraltar, monopolizing the Cornish tin trade. Thereafter the Etruscans were for the most part confined within the Tyrrhenian Sea.

Their landward expansion, however, was formidable. Between 550 and 500 B.C., their armies crossed the Tusco-Emilian Apennines and then began gradually subduing the Italic tribes of the Po Valley. They settled at Bologna, building a great city there, crossed over to the Adriatic, occupied Rimini and Ravenna, and established a thriving port at Spina, which became the entrepôt for valuable trade between the Greeks and the Celtic peoples beyond the Alps. Ancient Spina was, like Venice, built on piles amid a network of canals, and recent aerial photography has revealed the plan of the early city that covered some eight hundred and fifty acres. From this trade and their own exports Etruscan merchants became rich. Many Etruscan bronze and gold objects, as well as products of Greek origin, which were probably traded by the Etruscans to the people farther north, have been found in Switzerland and even Burgundy.

Southward they penetrated into Latium and Campania. The Latin tribes were weak and divided and the Etruscans had little difficulty in establishing control. They occupied the site of Rome, at that important strategic point where an easy crossing of the Tiber was guarded by the adjacent heights. It was they who made Rome a city. Later tradition recalled that the Etruscan dynasty of the Tarquins ruled Rome between 616 and 510 B.C. and that they were the last kings of ancient Rome before the founding of the Roman Republic. Before they were overthrown, Tyrrhenian soothsayers predicted that Rome would one day be 'the head of all Italy', and their predictions came to pass.

Etruria was never an empire united under a strong central government, but rather a loose federation of city-states each under its chief or lord, the *lucumon*. The lucumones were priest-kings, who ruled their native cities as chief judge and commander of the army. But their religious functions were equally important. On certain ritual occasions they appeared before the people riding in a chariot, drawn by white horses, and dressed as the god Tinia, king of the heavens. Like the god's, their own faces were coloured vermilion, and they wore long cloaks ornamented with stars. No doubt many of the most impressive early tombs that have been discovered were intended for the burial of lucumones.

Eventually the Etruscan monarchies were superseded by oligarchies, although the process was a gradual one. In Tarquinia and Cerveteri, kingship was abolished around 500 B.C., but in Veii it lingered on for decades more. Within the Etruscan league, which linked the major towns in a loose confederation, varying systems of government could exist side by side. There were twelve cities in the League, headed by a chief magistrate of the Etruscan nation, who was elected annually, but the confederation was never enabled to provide individual cities with reliable military protection against Rome.

Although they may have been less gifted as artists and innovators, the Romans had one vital quality that the Etruscans lacked – the capacity not only to rule but to win and retain the loyalty of the ruled. They also learned how to maintain power at the centre and to create a unified state that, as it expanded, did not break under stress. The Etruscan cities, though they fought bravely and often successfully against Rome, never managed to unite in effective common action against her. When Rome began her march to power, she annexed first one and then another piece of Etruscan territory. Then in the fourth century B.C. a new threat appeared from the north when the wild, semi-barbaric Gauls swept down into Italy.

At first the Etruscans fought the Gauls, later they tried to make allies of them against Rome, but the Romans, after suffering defeat and seeing their city burned by the invaders, eventually paid the Gauls to leave, as the Etruscans also had done. By that time the glory of Etruria was over, and not long afterward she had become, like the other Italian peoples, merely part of the Roman Republic.

The Romans learned, borrowed, and inherited much from their Etruscan neighbours and overlords before eliminating them as a cultural and political entity. Among other things, Etruscan elements survived in the trappings and insignia of office. The Roman toga originated as an Etruscan ceremonial garment and the sign of the fasces was originally carried by the Etruscan lictors when they marched in procession before their rulers; the bound rods of the fasces were for scourging, and the axe was a symbol of kingly power. The robe of office of the Etruscan rulers was purple, a colour which Romans adopted for a similar purpose and which, indeed, is still today an emblem of royalty. Together with these symbols the Romans also inherited the military 'triumphs' that followed a victory, and probably the gladiatorial shows and animal fights that gratified the lust for blood exhibited by Roman crowds in later days.

With this expansion of Roman power and influence Etruscan customs were overlaid by Roman. We can judge what sort of people the Etruscans were only by their earlier remains and by allusions to them in the later literature of other peoples. The latter, as we have earlier noted, were often prejudiced. In the fourth century B.C. the Greek historian Theopompus wrote,

> The Etruscans raise all children born without knowing to whom they belong. ... It is not shameful to the Etruscans to be seen not only preparing 'to do the thing', but also performing it. They are so far from considering this a disgrace that should, while the master of the house is making love, someone call on him, the visitor is told that he is doing this or that particular thing with no hesitation in specifying exactly which thing.

The same charming narrative goes on to describe how,

> When friends or relatives gather, this is their conduct: after they have finished drinking and are preparing to sleep, the slaves bring to them, while the lamps are still lighted, first prostitutes, by and by pretty young boys, then even the women married to those who took part in the festivities. They all engage in making love, some watching

one another, some isolating themselves by means of rattan screens set up around the couches, each couple wrapped in one cover.

There is some archaeological evidence to support this statement. The Etruscans did depict scenes of uninhibited pleasure on the walls of their tombs. The later Romans too had no scruples about painting orgiastic scenes on the walls of their villas, as at Pompeii. Unfortunately, since the Etruscans themselves have left us no memoirs to modify this picture of depravity as detailed in varying forms by Arnobius, Aristotle, and Plautus, we must either accept them or rely purely on the facts revealed by archaeology.

It would be disingenuous to ignore such stories altogether, since they have obtained wide currency. Theopompus may have had a weakness for romantic and exaggerated stories, yet most Greek writers stress the Etruscans' fondness for and indulgence in luxury – a point amply confirmed by the sumptuous

Engraved mirror back. The figures shown are probably dancers, although in antiquity it was rare for these to embrace.

Bronze warrior.

paraphernalia that accompanied them to their graves. As the tombs reveal, they were a life-loving people charged with such vigour as the Greeks had reason to complain of.

One sees the earlier Etruscans as sunburned sailors straining at the oars, while the sea foam crashes over the bulwarks and the look-out sights yet another island to explore or plunder; or marching smartly along their military roads in the triple formation of light, medium, and heavy infantry which the Romans copied in their legions. Their system of roads was as fine as anything achieved in Tuscany by the Romans centuries later – roads engineered to carry heavy traffic, well-drained, and laid out with tunnels and cuts. The lean and muscular armed warriors of grim and inscrutable visage, so familiar in early bronze and terracotta figures that have survived, as well

Chariot panel, showing an episode in the life of a mythological hero, perhaps Achilles.

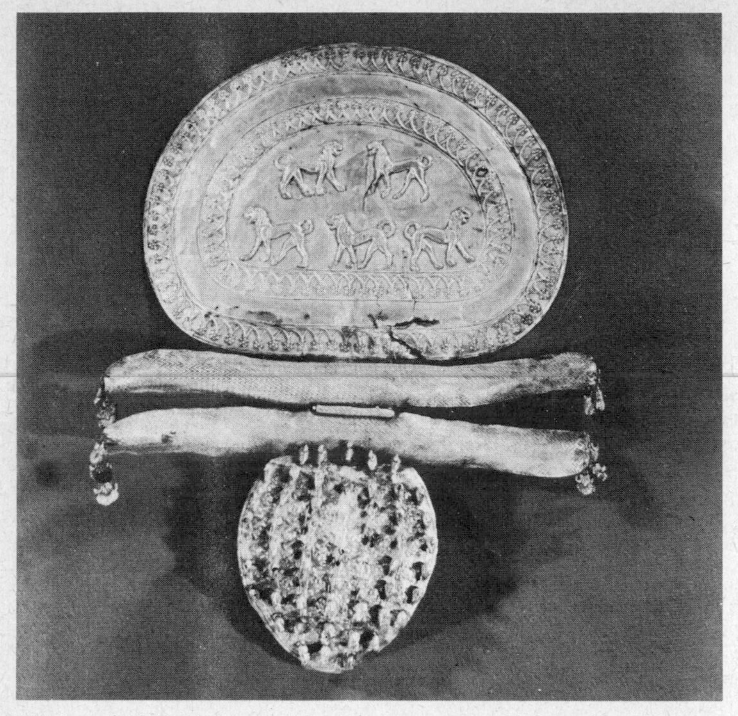

Discovered within the tomb of a princess, this dress pin [above] is made of gold, and decorated with the figures of five lions within a border of intertwined flowers. Its lower half is adorned with rows of winged lions, and with representations of ducks, beautifully modelled in gold. Upon the surface of the pin, thousands of tiny granules of gold are fused together to fashion the designs. This was a difficult technique in which the Etruscan goldsmiths excelled; it is also used to make the beard of the horned river god, Achelous [right].

as their resplendent and formidable chariots, speak eloquently for their military prowess.

One sees these early Etruscans mining copper and iron, trading with the barbarians of the north, and exchanging their raw materials for the exotic products of the east that they valued so highly, or for the gold and silver that their craftsmen fashioned into exquisite jewellery and ornaments. One sees their great fortified towns, mostly on hilltops – cities such as Volterra, which still retains part of its Etruscan walls,

including the famous Porta dell' Arco. These cities were usually laid out on a gridiron plan with two main intersecting thoroughfares, a system that the Romans also imitated in their military camps as well as in their cities. At the foundation of Rome, according to Plutarch, Romulus brought in Etruscans. The men from Tuscany

> prescribed all the details in accordance with certain sacred ordinances and writings, and taught them to him as in a religious rite. A circular trench was dug ... and in this were deposited first fruits of all things, the use of which was sanctioned by custom as good and by nature as necessary; and finally, every man brought a small portion of the soil of his native land and these were cast in among the first fruits and mingled with them. They call this trench, as they do the heavens, by the name of *mundus*. Then taking this as a centre, they marked out the city in a circle round it.

This shaft, at the centre of each Etruscan city, led directly to the underworld. It was covered by a great stone, called by the Romans 'the stone of souls', which was lifted up only on the days on which the dead were allowed to ascend among the living, or at the time when the first fruits were deposited underneath it as a harvest offering to the gods. The two main streets of the town crossed at this spot, dividing the area within the walls into quarters. This gridiron plan of the streets had a specific religious meaning; it reflected very closely the Etruscan view of the universe.

The Etruscans believed that the heavens above them were divided into quarters, each of which had an occult significance. In the north, at the very summit of the sky dwelt the king of the gods, Tinia. The east side of the heavens, on his left hand, was propitious. The west side, on his right, was less favourable, and the north-west corner of the heavens was the least fortunate of all, casting an especially malignant influence. Diviners further divided the heavens into sixteenths and assigned a meaning to each portion. Thus, it is no wonder that the Etruscans considered it necessary to search the heavens so carefully for omens.

Etruscan *haruspices*, or expert diviners, could read portents in thunderstorms and in the flight of birds, and find significance in the direction from which lightning came; they could foresee the future by examining the liver of a sheep which had been sacrificed especially for this purpose. At Piacenza, a bronze model of a liver was found. Like the heavens, it was divided up into sections, or 'houses', each of which was the residence of a particular god. This, it has been suggested, was a memory-aid for the haruspices; if they found an abnormality in part of the liver they were examining, they had only to refer to the bronze model to discover which divinity was concerned. The liver was chosen to represent the heavens because it was believed to be the seat of life.

The haruspices formed a special class, whose skill in the art of divination was the envy of other ancient nations. After the fall of Etruria, they continued to be honoured in Rome, and were frequently called upon to read omens for the emperors. Even as late as A.D. 408, when Rome was threatened with attack by a Visigoth army under Alaric, Pope Innocent I allowed them to try to conjure up lightning in an attempt to

Mirror showing a soothsayer examining the liver of a sacrificed beast for omens.

predict the future. (The future was bleak; the barbarians soon sacked the city.) It was only official members of the college of haruspices who could correctly interpret the intricate laws of divination, which had been inscribed in the ancient ritual books of Etruria and transmitted from generation to generation.

Besides the haruspices, there were other priests who officiated at religious ceremonies in the temples. The word *temple* itself is of Etruscan origin. It originally denoted that part of the heavens from which the diviner gathered his omens. The temples of Etruria were earthly counterparts of this sacred zone of heaven. Each temple was divided into three sections, one for each of the major gods of the Etruscan trinity; the building faced to the south, so that the image of Tinia could stand at the northern end of the sanctuary, the way the god himself lived at the northern end of the sky. The temple which the Tarquins constructed atop the capitol at Rome was similarly divided into three parts, and throughout their history the Romans followed this form whenever they built a capitoline temple within a newly founded city.

The Etruscans' houses, with a portico leading to a pillared courtyard from which frescoed rooms opened, were also copied by the Romans when they too had acquired a strong taste for luxurious living. Visitors to Pompeii and other Roman sites can see houses not unlike those in which the Etruscans lived and whose plan was reflected in Etruscan tombs. Even the Roman habit of dining from small, low tables while reclining on couches (a custom also known to the Greeks) was derived from Etruria. Such couches and banqueting scenes are depicted on the walls of Etruscan tombs as well as in the sarcophagi sculptures.

Music and the dance played a prominent role in Etruscan life. Aristotle is claimed to have said that the Tyrrhenians fought, kneaded dough, and beat their slaves to the sound of the flute. Other ancient writers tell us that music provided an inevitable accompaniment to sacrifices, banquets, boxing matches, and solemn ceremonies, and that the Etruscans even used music to aid them in snaring wild pigs and stags. Their painted tomb scenes of dancing to music have an abandon and

Red-figure vase of the fifth century B.C., showing a company of youths dancing.

frenetic ecstasy never approached in either Greek or Roman art. As D. H. Lawrence expressed it:

> This sense of vigorous, strong-bodied liveliness is characteristic of the Etruscans, and is somehow beyond art. You cannot think of art, but only of life itself, as if this were the very life of the Etruscans, dancing in their coloured wraps with massive yet exuberant naked limbs, ruddy from the air and the sea-light, dancing and fluting along through the little olive-trees, out in the fresh day.

The same spirit of warm, exhilarant life appears in the hunting scenes, especially in the idyllic fresco in the Tomb of Hunting and Fishing at Tarquinia. This has a delightful freshness and informality that is lacking in similar scenes from Egypt. A youth leans over the prow of a boat and drops

Tomb painting. The musician at the centre plays on the double flute, and one of his companions holds a lyre. Their dance may be taking place in a sacred laurel grove.

his line, while a dolphin playfully leaps near by. The oarsman is taking things easy in the stern, while other youths in the boat gesticulate to him. Overhead startled birds rise in hurried flight. There is no scene in any ancient fresco more enchanting than this; one can see what Lawrence means.

And yet there was another, darker side to the Etruscan character, an apparent fascination with pain, cruelty, and death particularly noticeable during the later and more decadent period of their history. Virtually all ancient authorities agree in describing the Etruscans as a highly religious people, in the sense that virtually every aspect of their life was prescribed by ritual regulations, from the founding of cities to burial of the dead. Unlike the Greeks, whose faith was liberally laced with scepticism and humour, the Etruscan

Fresco at Tarquinia.

mind was disciplined by strict and fearful regard for the divine powers and a constant anxiety lest by neglect of omens, signs, and rites these powers should be offended.

The Greeks also used divination, but their philosophic spirit prevented them from allowing their lives to be completely dominated by religious doctrine or practice. The Romans later also adopted certain Etruscan religious customs, including divination by the examination of entrails, but they too distinguished between secular and religious matters. The Etruscans did not. Their minds appear to have been imprisoned within a rigid framework of doctrine, which had been revealed to their ancestors and which was immutable. This doctrine was not concerned with problems of ethical or moral conduct. The correct interpretation of signs and the due observance of the appropriate rites were apparently, to the Etruscans, ends in themselves.

This tomb fresco shows two powerful wrestlers struggling against each other during a ritual contest for the dead. The three bowls standing beside them may be the winner's prize. The two priests at left are referees; one of them carries a *lituus*, or curved staff, to signify his office.

The Etruscans had numerous gods, some of whom were adopted Hellenic deities, but the principal triad consisted of Tinia, Uni, and Menerva, whose Roman analogues were Jupiter, Juno, and Minerva. But there were also demons, spirits of horror and death, and as the centuries passed these were depicted more and more frequently in the tombs. One of them, the sinister Charun, who obviously took his name from the Greek ferryman of the Styx, had a horse's ears and a beaked nose, and was armed with a large mallet. With a body the colour of decaying flesh he seems a veritable embodiment of a scene of human sacrifice. The figure of Charun was shown towering over the victim, his demon's face painted an eerie blue, and holding an enormous hammer in his hand.

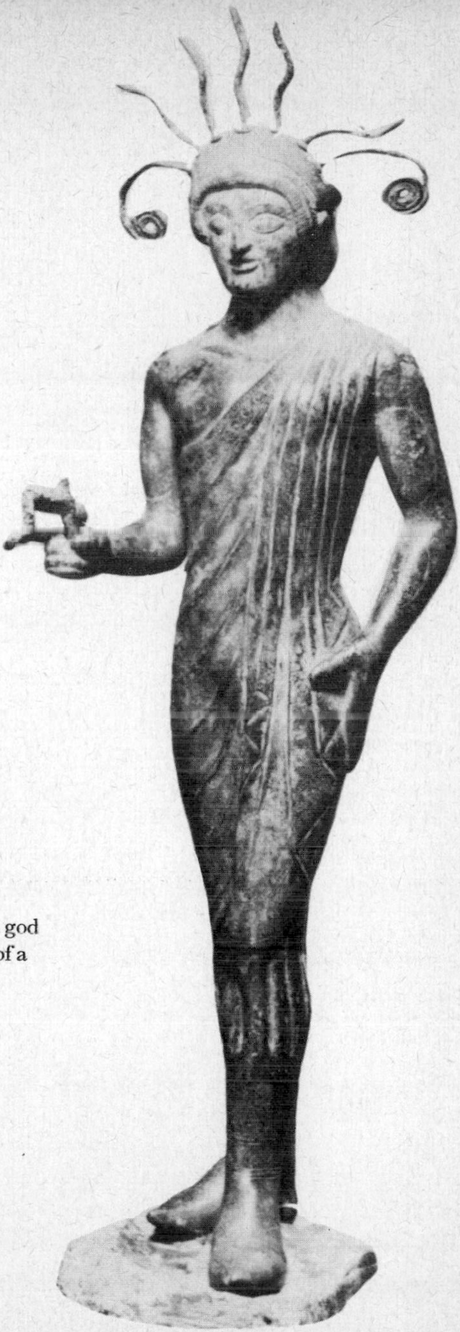

Tinia, related to the Greek god Zeus, holding the remains of a thunderbolt.

After the fifth century B.C. Etruscan funerary paintings emphasize scenes of massacre, torture, and violent death. The grimmest of these pictures depict what appear to have been the ritual 'sports' that accompanied Etruscan funeral ceremonies. One wall painting shows a battle to the death between two Etruscan gladiators; another the sacrifice of the Trojan captives who were killed at the tomb of Patroclus by Achilles. Some have suggested that such horrors may only depict the sufferings of the damned in an Etruscan hell, but as Etruscan religion does not appear to have contained any doctrine of sin and punishment this is unlikely. It is probably true, however, that such scenes represented ritual performances in accordance with the Etruscan religious doctrine, unlike the later pointless and brutal spectacles that were staged in the days of imperial Rome.

Curiosity about pain, violence, and death, always present in the darker recesses of the human mind, may have been magnified by the Etruscans until it developed into a morbid obsession. What caused this we cannot be certain, but it may have been a succession of military defeats, reinforcing a belief already impressed by Etruscan religion that as in the life of man, so in that of peoples there is birth, maturity, and death. In one of the Etruscan religious documents, the *Libri fatales* (the books of destiny), which is known from Roman writings, human life is given a span of twelve times seven years (seven often occurs as a sacred number in primitive religion). The Etruscans also believed that their nation had a life of ten *saecula* (a variable period of eighty to one hundred and twenty years), after which it would disappear. Perhaps, as the Etruscan hegemony gradually collapsed under the alternate hammer-blows of Romans and Gauls, the Etruscans saw in this the inexorable workings of destiny. No doubt, as the time ordained for the death of their nation drew closer, Etruscan soldiers went out to war with little heart for battle, little expectation of victory. This fatalism may be why, during the period of their decline, the Etruscans laid increasing emphasis on the more sombre aspects of their religion. It may be so, but we do not know.

Certainly from the earliest times they had been deeply concerned for the welfare of their dead, burying them in tombs of increasing richness and beauty, decorating the walls with painted frescoes, and equipping these mausoleums – which, like those of ancient Egypt, were Houses of Eternity – with everything the dead would need in the afterlife. But after the fifth century B.C. the gay scenes of hunting and feasting and dancing become fewer, and are replaced by more solemn subjects such as those described above. The sculptured figures on the sarcophagi also change, becoming soft, flabby, and indolent; they loll on cushions, and hold wine cups, while on their faces is a curious expression, neither wholly joyous nor wholly melancholic, but an expression resigned, detached, and enigmatic.

By 250 B.C. Etrúria was part of the Roman political system, though for a time it still retained its individual character. One hundred years later, throughout the land funeral inscriptions were being written in Latin, and by the time of Christ the Etruscan language had died out, except among the country people. Roman cities rose on the sites of such Etruscan towns as Tarquinia, Perugia, and Arezzo, to be replaced in turn by medieval and modern buildings. Some Etruscan towns were deserted and never reoccupied, and even these were plundered of their stone, so that today little survives. But the cemeteries – the huge underground cities of the dead at Cerveteri, Tarquinia, Vulci, and many other sites – remain. Though thousands of tombs have been ransacked and their precious wall paintings left to decay, others are still intact. As recently as 1957, the Italian archaeologist Carlo M. Lerici began using electronic methods to detect tomb sites, and then examined still-buried tombs by boring a narrow hole in the roof, lowering an automatic camera that could be revolved around 360 degrees, and photographing the interiors. In this way he discovered the first painted and decorated tombs found at Tarquinia since 1892; one of these contained a lively depiction of various athletes leaping, running, and tossing the discus. At Vulci a large tomb was discovered containing an elaborate sarcophagus with scenes of different character carved in high relief – a massacre of maidens watched by a male and a female deity. No doubt more tombs will be found, of which a few may yet remain intact. Etruscology is now as precise a discipline as other branches of archaeology, and new scientific methods have replaced the careless plundering of former years.

We may one day succeed in understanding the Etruscan language, though all known examples are short inscriptions, mostly funerary; the longest, a religious document, is of only fifteen hundred words. Possibly the long-debated question of Etruscan origins may finally be settled. Until these problems are solved, and perhaps even after they are, the Etruscans themselves will retain their mystery. We can enjoy their vital, exuberant art, admire the craftsmanship of their jewellers, metalworkers, sculptors, and painters. But they themselves continue to remain apart from us. Across twenty-five centuries their sensitive, worldly faces regard us with ironical amusement, half-smiling, as if they held some secret. They remain one of the great enigmas of history.

Guide to Further Reading

CRETE

Chadwick J., *The Decipherment of Linear B*, Penguin Books, 1961
Cottrell L., *The Bull of Minos*, Evans, 1953
Evans, Sir A., *The Palace of Minos*, Macmillan, London, 1921–35
Hutchinson, R.W., *Prehistoric Crete*, Penguin Books, 1962
Pendlebury, J.D.S., *The Archaeology of Crete*, Methuen, 1965
Pendlebury, J.D.S., *The Palace of Minos* (Guide), Max Parrish, London, 1954

MYCENAE

Blegen, C.W., *The Mycenaean Age*, Cincinnati, 1962
Cottrell, L., *The Lion Gate*, Evans, 1963
Marinatos, S., *Crete and Mycenae*, Thames & Hudson, 1960
Mylonas, G.E., *Ancient Mycenae*, London, 1957
Page, D., *History and the Homeric Iliad*, Berkeley, California, 1959
Palmer, L., *Mycenaeans and Minoans*, Faber & Faber, 1961
Wace, A.J.B., *The Arrival of the Greeks*, Viking, 1954
Wace, A.J.B., *Mycenae*, Princeton, 1949

ANATOLIA

Blegen, C.W., *Troy* (3 vols.), Princeton, 1950
Gurney, O.R., *The Hittites*, Penguin Books, 1952
Lloyd, S., *Early Anatolia*, Penguin Books, 1956
Schliemann, H., *Ilios: The City and Country of the Trojans*, London, 1880

THE ETRUSCANS

Bloch, R., *The Etruscans*, Thames & Hudson, 1958
Soustelle, J., *Daily Life of the Etruscans*, Weidenfeld & Nicolson, London, 1961

Acknowledgements

Grateful acknowledgment is made for permission to quote from the following works: Carl Blegen, 'Excavations at Pylos 1939', *American Journal of Archaeology*, vol. XLIII, no. 4, 1939. C.W. Ceram, *The Secret of the Hittites*, Alfred A. Knopf Inc., N.Y. John Chadwick, *The Decipherment of Linear B*, Cambridge University Press, N.Y. Edward Chiera, *They Wrote on Clay*, University of Chicago Press, copyright 1938 The University of Chicago. *Diodorus Siculus*, vols. I and II; Dionysius of Halicarnassus, *The Roman Antiquities*; passages reprinted by permission of the publishers from the Loeb Classical Library, Cambridge, Mass.: Harvard University Press. Sir Arthur Evans, *The Palace of Minos at Knossos*, reprinted 1963 Agathon Press Inc., N.Y. Joan Evans, *Time and Chance*, Longmans, Green & Co. Ltd, London. *Kingship and the Gods*, University of Chicago Press, copyright 1948 The University of Chicago. Gustave Glotz, *Aegean Civilization*, Routledge & Kegan Paul Ltd, London. *Herodotus: The Histories*, trans. Aubrey de Selincourt, Penguin Books Ltd (by permission of David Higham Associates Ltd, London). Alain Hus, *The Etruscans*, trans. Jeanne Unger Duell, Grove Press Inc., N.Y. E. O. James, *The Ancient Gods*, G.P. Putnam's Sons. D.H. Lawrence, *Etruscan Places*, by permission of The Viking Press Inc., all rights reserved. Miriam Lichtheim, 'The Songs of Harpers', *Journal of Near Eastern Studies*, vol. IV, no. 3, 1945, The University of Chicago. J.D.S. Pendlebury, *The Archaeology of Crete*, Methuen & Co. Ltd. James B. Pritchard, ed. *Ancient Near Eastern Texts Relating to the Old Testament*, copyright 1955 Princeton University Press, Princeton. Sir Osbert Sitwell, *Escape With Me*, Macmillan & Co., London (by permission of David Higham Associates Ltd). Alan Wace, *Mycenae: An Archaeological History and Guide*, copyright 1949 Princeton University Press.

PICTURE CREDITS

The source of each picture is listed below. Its title or description appears after the page number, which is in italic type, and is followed by the original location, where possible, and the present location. Where two or more pictures appear on one page, the references are separated by dashes.

Frontispiece Lion Gate, Mycenae. (Robert E. Ginna) *10* Horns of consecration, Knossos. (Erich Lessing, Magnum) *21* The queen's apartments, Knossos. (Hirmer) *22* Bull's-head rhyton from Knossos. Archaeological Museum, Herakleion (Hassia) *24* Throne room, palace of Minos, Knossos. (Robert E. Ginna) *27* Fresco of 'La Parisienne' from Knossos. Archaeological Museum, Herakleion (J. Powell) *28–9* Restored bull-leapers fresco from Knossos. Archaeological Museum, Herakleion (Hirmer) *30–1* Audience fresco from Knossos, copy. (Ashmolean Museum, Oxford) *33* Gold ring from Isopata. Archaeological Museum, Herakleion (J. Powell) *35* Snake goddess from Knossos. Archaeological Museum, Herakleion (J. Powell) *37* 'Priest-King' fresco from Knossos, restored. Archaeological Museum, Herakleion (Hassia) *38* Double axe from cave near Knossos. (Museum of Fine Arts, Boston) *40* Dolphin fresco. Knossos (Hassia) *41* Bathtub from Pachyammos. Archaeological Museum, Herakleion (Hassia) *42* House plaque from Knossos. Archaeological Museum, Herakleion (J. Powell) *43* Vase from Phaistos. Archaeological Museum, Herakleion (Hassia) *44* Palace of Mallia. (Robert Descharnes) *46* Gold pendant from Mallia. Archaeological Museum, Herakleion (J. Powell) *49* Goddess from Knossos. Archaeological Museum, Herakleion (Hassia) *51* Chieftain's Cup from Hagia Triada. Archaeological Museum, Herakleion (Hassia) *53* Statuette from Tylissos. Archaeological Museum, Herakleion (Hirmer) *54* Group of women and lyre player from Palaikastro. Archaeological Museum, Herakleion (Hassia) *56–7* Ivory acrobat from Knossos. Archaeological Museum, Herakleion (Hassia) *57* Statuette of acrobat on bull. (E.G. Spencer-Churchill Collection, Gloucester) *58–9* Sarcophagus painting from Hagia Triada. Archaeological Museum, Herakleion (J. Powell) *64* Lion Gate, Mycenae. (Robert E. Ginna) *68* Gold signet ring from Tiryns. National Archaeological Museum, Athens (Hirmer) *69* Dagger blade, Mycenae, detail. National Archaeological Museum, Athens (J. Powell) *72* Mycenaean vase. National Archaeological Museum, Athens *73* Ivory warrior from Delos. Delos Museum (French School at Athens) *74* Fresco from Tiryns. National Archaeological Museum, Athens *78* Mask, Mycenae. National Archaeological Museum, Athens *79* Rock crystal dish, Mycenae. National Archaeological Museum, Athens – Gold cup, Mycenae. National Archaeological Museum, Athens *80* Mask, Mycenae. National Archaeological Museum, Athens (J. Powell) *84* Gold cup from Vaphio. National Archaeological Museum, Athens *85* Gold cup, and detail of gold cup, from Vaphio. National Archaeological Museum, Athens (Hirmer) *86* Warrior Vase, Mycenae. National Archaeological Museum, Athens *89* Octopus ornament, Mycenae. National Archaeological Museum, Athens (Hirmer) *94* Statuette. Courtesy of the Brooklyn Museum, the Guennol Collection *98* Line drawing of Egyptian relief of Sea Peoples. Original at Medinet Habu.

Oriental Institute Publications, Chicago, 1930, vol. 8 *101* Drawing of battle at Deper. Original on Ramesseum, Thebes. W. Wreszinski, *Atlas zur altägyptischen Kulturgeschichte*, Leipzig, 1923–36 *103* Tablet from Kultepe. Ankara (Turkish Embassy, London) *105* Lion Gate, Boghazkoy. (J. Powell) *106* Gate figure from Boghazkoy. Ankara (Hirmer) *107* Relief, Yazilikaya. (J. Powell) *108* Rock relief from Yazilikaya. (J. Powell) *109* Egyptian painting of Syrian traders, copy. Original at Beni Hasan. C.R. Lepsius, *Denkmaeler aus Aegypten und Aethiopien*, Berlin, 1849–59 *112* Hittite stag. Ankara (Yan) *119* Marriage stele from Abu Simbel. (Oriental Institute, University of Chicago) *120* Relief of acrobats from Alaja Huyuk. Ankara (Hirmer) *121* Hunting relief from Malatya. Ankara (Hirmer) *122* Vase fragment from Boghazkoy. Ankara (Hirmer) *123* Five-sided stamp. (Ashmolean Museum, Oxford) *125* Weather god stele from Babylon. Archaeological Museums of Istanbul (Yan) *128* Knife scabbard from Byblos. National Museum, Beirut (Thames & Hudson) *129* Double axe from Byblos. National Museum, Beirut (courtesy Thames & Hudson, *Dawn of Civilisation*) *131* Mother goddess ivory from Minet el Beida. Louvre (Archives Photographiques) *132* From a terracotta relief of Phrygian warriors, near Boghazkoy. Ankara (J. Powell) *134* Tarkondemos seal. (Ashmolean Museum, Oxford) *136* Turms from Veii. Villa Giulia (Scala) *142* Cinerary urn. Villa Giulia (David Lees) *143* Tomb of stucco reliefs, Cerveteri. (Alinari) *144* Bronze and silver helmet from Todi. Villa Giulia (David Lees) *145* Sarcophagus from Cerveteri. Villa Giulia (Kate Lewin) *146* Chimera from Arezzo. Museo Archeologico, Florence *147* Gorgon from Veii. Villa Giulia (Scala) *149* Ploughing group from Arezzo. Villa Giulia (Pallottino and Hurlimann, *The Art of the Etruscans*, Thames & Hudson) *153* Mirror. Antikensammlungen, Munich (Jean-Pierre Sudre) *154* Warrior. Musei Civici, Perugia (Dimitri Kessel, courtesy *Life* Magazine) *155* Side panel from Etruscan chariot. (Metropolitan Museum of Art, Rogers Fund, 1903) *156* Pin from Cerveteri. Museo Etrusco del Vaticana (Dimitri Kessel, courtesy *Life* Magazine) *157* Achelous pendant. Louvre *159* Mirror from Vulci. Museo Etrusco del Vaticana *161* Vase from Campagnano. Villa Giulia (Dimitri Kessel, courtesy *Life* Magazine) *162* Painting from Tomb of the Leopards, Tarquinia. (Alinari) *163* Painting from Tomb of Hunting and Fishing, Tarquinia. (*Arte Etrusca*, Silvana Editoriale d'Arte) *164* Painting from Tomb of the Augurs, Tarquinia. (David Lees) *165* Tinia. (Fitzwilliam Museum, Cambridge).

Index

NOTE. *Page numbers in italics refer to illustrations or their captions*

More about Penguins

If you have enjoyed reading this book you may wish to know that *Penguin Book News* appears every month. It is an attractively illustrated magazine containing a complete list of books published by Penguins and still in print, together with details of the month's new books. A specimen copy will be sent free on request.

Penguin Book News is obtainable from most bookshops; but you may prefer to become a regular subscriber at 3s. for twelve issues. Just write to Dept EP, Penguin Books Ltd, Harmondsworth, Middlesex, enclosing a cheque or postal order, and you will be put on the mailing list.

Some Pelicans are described on the following pages.

Note: *Penguin Book News* is not
available in the U.S.A., Canada or Australia.

The Aztecs of Mexico

George C. Vaillant

Dr George Vaillant was that rara avis, a great specialist who could make his speciality as interesting to the layman as it was to himself. For many years curator of Mexican archaeology at the American Museum of Natural History, and acknowledged an outstanding authority on the early civilizations of Mexico and Central America, in this book he wrote what is still the most important account of the birth and death of one of the world's great civilizations.

In the eleventh century the Aztecs arrived in Mexico from the north. Even today their speech is much like that spoken by the Indians of Oregon and Montana. In less than a hundred years, rising on the ruins of the older Mexican cultures, they developed an extraordinary indigenous civilization. Here is the strange story of the rise, and of the even swifter fall under the impact of Cortes and his followers. Dr Vaillant vividly re-creates the Aztec way of life. In one fascinating chapter he takes his reader to the great Aztec city, Tenochtitlan, now Mexico City, in the days of the height of the Aztec power, and wanders with him through the town. We learn not only the history of the Aztecs and how their society was organized, but how the children went to school, modes of dress, and many interesting aspects of an ancient daily life.

'One does not know which to admire most, the care with which the details are assembled or the imagination which has constructed cultural and political history out of them. No reader of *The Conquest of Mexico* should miss this book' – *Time and Tide*

Ancient Iraq

Georges Roux

Of the great civilizations which flourished for over three thousand years between the Tigris and the Euphrates, little seemed to remain: ages of decline tended to obliterate almost every trace of the art, science, and literature of the Sumerians, Akkadians, Babylonians, and Assyrians. During the last century, however, there has been an unceasing effort on the part of archaeologists to uncover the monuments and texts which reveal the history and civilization of the region once called Mesopotamia.

Ancient Iraq is the first full political, cultural, and economic history to attempt to cover the whole of Mesopotamia from the days of prehistory to the dawn of the Christian era. Dr Roux describes the empires, dynasties, and religions of each millennium and suggests something of the splendour of Babylon before its capture by Cyrus. That so vast a subject makes such absorbing reading is due not only to the inevitable fascination of the past, but to the light, yet exact, touch of a talented historian.

The Ancient Civilizations of Peru

J. Alden Mason

Our detailed knowledge of the people of pre-Columbian Peru has grown enormously since 1940. Many expeditions have made excavations and published their reports. Regions archaeologically unknown hitherto have yielded their secrets, and far more is known of all of them. Especially is this true of the cultures that preceded the Inca whom Pizarro found and conquered in one of the great adventures of history. Four thousand years before his day, radiocarbon analyses now permit us to state with confidence, simple fishermen-hunters on the coast were beginning the long climb towards the extraordinary blend of communism and monarchy that was the Inca empire. Our concepts of the latter and of its history also have been altered somewhat by recent studies. This book presents a summary of our present knowledge and point of view regarding the development and nature of these past civilizations and their fascinating and diversified country, with sixty-four pages of plates.

Archaic Egypt

W. B. Emery

Between 1936 and 1956 archaeological discoveries at Sakkara, the necropolis of ancient Memphis, have produced evidence which has caused historians to revise many of their previous conceptions of Egyptian civilization of the first two dynasties (3200–2780 B.C.). The origins of the Egypt of the Pharaohs still remain obscure, but the new material uncovered by the pick of the excavator shows that the people of the Nile Valley at that remote period enjoyed a far higher degree of culture than has hitherto been recognized. Architecture and the arts had reached a degree of excellence which in some ways was hardly surpassed when the full flower of Pharaonic civilization was in bloom.

The aim of this book is to put before the reader a general survey of what we now know, through these recent discoveries, of the cultural achievements of the great people who lived on the banks of the Nile nearly five thousand years ago. While in no sense a textbook this absorbing study will make an equal appeal to the student and to the layman.

The Ancient Explorers

M. Cary and E. H. Warmington

Two eminent scholars – both professors in the University of London – collaborated in the writing of this volume, which remains a standard work on ancient travel and discovery. Concerned with the actual journeys made rather than with the geographical speculations of ancient scholars, they tell how, before Arabic expansion closed the gates of the Mediterranean Sea, men had coasted Western Europe and penetrated the continent south of the Danube and Rhine, sailed from Suez to Canton and probed deeply into Asia, and – even if they failed to circumnavigate Africa – had been as far as Sierra Leone and Port Delgado. They describe, too, the objects of these journeys, the crude equipment of sailors, and the scanty geographical knowledge on which they proceeded.

In this 'Hakluyt' of the ancient world one reads – often with surprise – of Greeks in India and Romans in China, of the account of the source of the Nile given by one Diogenes, and of Pytheas's extended visit to the boorish inhabitants of Britain. And it is clear that the Great Age of Discovery, in the fifteenth and sixteenth centuries, was heavily indebted to these more ancient explorers.

The Penguin Book of Lost Worlds *Volume 1*

Leonard Cottrell

While each of these volumes will happily stand by itself, the fascination of the past is not so easy to deny. The reader who has chosen the second volume for some interest of his own will soon return to buy the preceding one. In the first volume he will find the full story of Egypt as we now know it; of Mesopotamia, from the Sumerians to the fall of Babylon; and of the Harappa civilization which arose in the Indus Valley some four thousand years ago.